From the Weaver's Loom

Reflections on the Sundays and Feasts

From the Weaver's Loom

Reflections on the Sundays and Feasts

Donald Hanson

Resurrection Press
Mineola, New York

Nihil obstat: Rev. Msgr. John A. Alesandro, S.T.L., J.C.D.
                   Censor Librorum
                   May 31, 1990

Imprimatur: Most Reverend John R. McGann, D.D.
                 Bishop of Rockville Centre
                 June 5, 1990

First published in 1990 by   Resurrection Press
                              P.O. Box 248
                              Williston Park, NY 11596

ISBN 1-878718-01-0

Library of Congress Catalog Card Number 90-070774

Cover design: William Hanson

Printed in the United States of America by Faith Printing.

Zoo zit en zingt er menig man,
vroemorgens op 't getouwe, om, van
goen drom, te maken
langlijdend lijwaadlaken.

De wever zingt, zijn' webbe deunt;
de la klabakt, 't getouwe dreunt
en lijzig varen
de spoelen heen, in 't garen.

—————————

Thus sit and sing the worker may,
before the loom, at peep of day,
from woof to shape
longlasting linen drape.

The weaver sings, his tissue tunes;
the batten clatters, the frame booms;
and swiftly tread
the spools along the thread.

Guido Gezelle
(1830-1899)
Flemish poet and priest

Antiphon

The seat of the Catholic University of Louvain has been located, almost since its foundation in 1425, in the ancient hall of the medieval cloth workers' guild. This may seem an unlikely place to set up a university, but not to one who journeyed there for some months of theological reflection and restoration, as the author did in the Spring of 1990. The appropriateness of this alliance between drapers and theologians is suggested by the task which occupied him during that time, the editing and re-shaping of the book you have in hand. The reflections that follow began their life as parish homilies. They are, therefore, modest attempts at theological interpretation.

Here is the connection between cloth weaving and theology. Liturgical preaching attempts to weave together threads of various textures and hues: an understanding of the appointed scripture passages; the rhythm and tone of each Sunday and feast within the warp and weft of the calendar; the nubs of people's struggles, hopes and dreams; the highlights of insight, image and tune from poets, writers, theologians. The task is to produce a kind of craft work: to make a useful thing, and one hand-wrought; to make it lovingly and make it well; and, just occasionally, to make it beautiful. Pastoral theology, which is what preaching aspires to be, is an artisan's endeavor. It is concrete, occasional and homely. When it succeeds it will help, inspire, encourage. These then are some patches from the weaver's loom. You may try them on if you like.

Thanks must go to the parish communities of St. Raymond, East Rockaway and St. Agnes Cathedral, Rockville Centre, New York, in which most of these reflections were born, and to the parishioners and friends who provided both yarn and encouragement to the weaver. Thanks to Bishop John McGann who generously granted me the sabbatical in which it was finished; and to the community of The American College, Louvain, Belgium, particularly to Dr. John A. Dick, who offered a place of hospitality and peace in which to work. Lastly, thanks to my editor, Nancy Benvenga, who prompted, encouraged and saw it through.

Contents

ADVENT

First Sunday of Advent: Darkness and light

"O shepherd of Israel, . . . shine forth."

Advent always arrives in the nick of time, a short season for the short space between Fall and Winter. Advent, clad in darkling blue or somber purple, is a perfect fit for the frenzied chaos which comes between Thanksgiving and Christmas. Advent arrives just when we need to be saved from ourselves.

Not so Lent. Lent is a major undertaking. Lent, if you make but the least effort to observe it, hangs on you like a bad cold: seven weeks of serious fasting, plus one filled with austere and beautiful liturgy, the *coup de grace* to put you out of your misery. Lent hangs around till it is sure the old man is dead.

But Advent is brief and to the point. No dramatic ash-smearing; no warm-ups or limbering exercises here. Bang, the candle is lit and we're into it! Advent begins with a start, like being plunged into cold water. It is sudden; brutal as the cruel clock that summons us to work and to the world each morning. And if we may believe the gospel, it is a talking clock which nags: "Stay awake! . . . Be on watch! . . . Be on guard!" It is relentless. There is no snooze bar; no dream machine with a few extra minutes' reward for a well directed tap. Like the drill sergeant in boot camp, Advent gives no choice. Rise and shine! Up and at 'em!

Advent suits our darker moods. The days are short; the light is going. So, in the words of Dylan Thomas, for four weeks we "do not go gentle into that good night, [but]

1

rage against the dying of the light." Perhaps darkness and light are the best emblems for our situation. As we veer toward the winter solstice we know that the creeping darkness is all because mother earth has turned her face away from the sun. In the fierce heat of summer the earth vaunted herself, declaring to the sun, "I don't need you. I can manage quite well without you. Thank you very much." And now we are paying the price. At least, this is the way I imagine our ancestors imagining it in the days before telescopes.

Advent is a perfect emblem for our rebellion against God. The great tale of our first parents is recapitulated in us year after year. On the cusp of winter we discover ourselves outside the garden, driven away from the warmth and the life. And all because we thought ourselves self-sufficient and better than we are. "If you eat this fruit you shall become like gods." So we tasted, and here is the result. We said, "I can make it on my own. Thank you very much." And here we are shivering from the cold and buttoning up against the damp.

Advent is a cry in the night, a shriek against the cold, a shout to ward away death. Advent is a sharp, strong prayer. "O that you would rend the heavens and come down." "Lord, *make us* turn to you, let us see your face and we shall be saved." There is nothing fanciful or "make-believe" about the Advent mood. We are not pretending to be living in Old Testament days waiting for the birth of the Messiah whose appearance started our watches running and our calendar countdown. The question for us is simply, will he come again and when? Is he with us now and where? Will he make his presence felt to save us?

Advent is supposed to be the beginning of the Church year. No! It is the beginning of the end. Advent confronts our real fears for the future. Like an unseen hand it whirls our heads around and forces us to look at what we would not see. It makes us face front and behold the future with open eyes. Shutting the eyes when the scary parts come is not allowed in Advent. Jesus says, "Be constantly on the watch! . . . Look around you!" Advent sticks

2

our nose in it; demands we be responsible for the mess we've made.

Yet, Advent offers us an alternative, else it would not be "gospel." It is a winter break not unlike the ones advertised in the Sunday newspaper travel section. Advent has not the time for cruises, but it can book a quick flight into the sun. All we must do is imitate the earth and turn again toward that sun, incline the axis of our life toward the true center of the world, that is, toward Jesus Christ. We must turn our backs on the dark and the deeds of darkness. We must turn toward the light and turn toward the warmth. "He will strengthen you till the end, so that you will be blameless on the day of our Lord Jesus Christ." "O shepherd of Israel, shine forth." The Sun of Righteousness will shine for those who seek his light. Let us call out to him: "Lord Jesus, Son of God, have mercy on me a sinner." "Come, Lord Jesus!"

Second Sunday of Advent: Good beginnings

"Here begins the gospel of Jesus Christ, the Son of God."

"It was the best of times. It was the worst of times." "Long ago in a galaxy far away." Perhaps you remember those opening lines. A good beginning is important, especially in an epic novel or motion picture. Today we begin the gospel of Mark, which we shall continue to read for a year.

"Here begins the gospel of Jesus Christ, the Son of God." Perhaps it is not as literary as *A Tale of Two Cities*, or as naively self-important as the prologue to *Star Wars*, but as a beginning it will serve. It has a certain directness and bravery. It sounds rather like the opening chant of the childhood game, "Ready or not—here I come."

Mark is very direct and comes straight to the point.

Unlike Matthew and Luke he has no infancy narrative. The birth and childhood of Jesus seemingly do not interest him. It is the adult Christ he wishes to present, and that with all its force and fullest impact. So he uses John the Baptist as his foil. There can be no doubt that John was a real attention-getter. Mark tells us that "John was clothed in camel's hair and wore a leather belt around his waist. His food was grasshoppers and wild honey." You can almost smell him, even at a distance of two millennia, so vivid, so bizarre is he. Yet he plays his role and plays it well.

John is a pointer. In modern campaign politics he would be the advance man gathering the crowd. In theatrical terms, he is not the main attraction but the trailer for the next feature — a teaser meant to arouse attention and build interest. In many ways John is the last of the Old Testament prophets, even though he appears in the opening pages of the New Testament. He is an odd-ball, an ascetic. He preaches a disturbing and discomfiting message and is hated on account of it, though he was neither without success nor followers. John says, "One more powerful than I is to come after me. . . . I have baptized you in water; he will baptize you in the Holy Spirit." It is, of course, Jesus he is speaking of. Jesus, the Son of God, as Mark announces him.

We stand at the threshold of a new year of grace, the beginning of yet another reading of this gospel. Can we allow it to speak to us again? Can we reread it once more with pleasure as we would a favorite novel? Can we treat ourselves to another viewing of this greatest saga, still so full of interest and excitement?

For if we read and listen, it will never be just the same old story but ever new and ever surprising. For it is a story that is powerful, captivating and fully able to transform us. It is the tale of "one more powerful" than we (or John) imagined, and it can change us — even us, so weary and jaded.

"Here begins the gospel of Jesus Christ, the Son of God." "May the words of the gospel wipe away our sins."

Third Sunday of Advent: The right questions

"There is one among you whom you do not recognize. . ."

John the Baptist gets the third degree, like a teenager home late from a date. "Where were you? Who were you with? Where did you go? What did you do?" And while the teenager may be mute, evasive or try to put the right spin on her answers, John is perfectly plain-spoken. I am not the Messiah. I am not Elijah. The prophet? No. I am "a voice in the desert, crying out: Make straight the way of the Lord!" But there is more at stake here than the nervous inquiries of a worried parent. This is a different kind of questioning.

Something curious happens when questioning passes from keen interest to interrogation. The attitude of the questioner is likely to interfere with the discovery of truth. The question acquires a distinctive edge in which it is assumed the truth is already known. The question becomes narrow in the wrong way, closing itself off to surprise and discovery. The answer becomes a kind of password, a signal of recognition and assurance for the interrogator. Here, the priests and Levites are clearly agents of an interested power. John has come to the attention of the state security forces, so operatives have been dispatched to observe and interview him. They are hoping he will "help them with their inquiries," so that they in turn can check out of the flea-bitten Bethany Hotel and return to the fleshpots of Jerusalem. Forgive them if they seem a little impolite. They want this to be a routine investigation. They need to close the case.

John, who is never ambiguous, is straightforward with them, yet gives an enigmatic answer. He quotes the oracle of Isaiah about the voice crying out in the desert. The sense of it is not "I'm delivering the message but I might as well be in the desert for all the heed I'm given." Rather, in Isaiah the voice in the desert is the welcome word addressed to the exiles, the word of liberation to the prisoners, the healing word to the broken, the saving word to those who are perishing. The word of John, incomprehensible to the minions of the regime, and dangerous therefore, is salvation to those who really need and want it. And yet this saving word is offered even to the interrogators. John is not trying to be clever with them, he is not teasing them or trying to throw them off the track. The good news is offered to all, to the good and the bad, the ins and the outs, the haves and the have-nots. But in fact, it is only the brokenhearted, the lowly, the captives who have the least interest in it.

The men from Jerusalem question further. What has he been up to at the Jordan? What is all this baptizing about? They want to know if it is a subversive activity. What does it mean? Of course, they cannot begin to understand, so their paranoia is inflamed. It is easy for them, easy for the regime, to believe there is danger. They give the appearance of strength through strong-arm tactics and terror, but terror is always the signal of their weakness. The prophet is dangerous because the powers that be are insecure and jealous of their authority.

Again John answers with a word both hopeful and provoking. "There is one among you whom you do not recognize — the one to come after me — the strap of whose sandal I am not worthy to unfasten." Now, this is really provocative. Suddenly they see that John is not the end of it. There is somebody else, a head man, an organization, a cadre. This is what they likely hear, but this is not what he means. He means the savior is already present, a reason for rejoicing. To the interrogators this is not cause for joy but worry; it is not to be simple after all. We hear no more of them. Presumably they go back to Jerusalem to report to their masters. Another page for the dossier. But how stupid they are; how blind, and what a chance missed!

Our questions of God equally demand answers, but we must really want answers, really listen for them and not merely look to shore up our own prejudices. The good news is, "There is one among you whom you do not recognize. . ." The savior has appeared and is already in our midst. We must not be so blind as to apprehend the wrong man. We must not let him slip through our fingers because of bungled detective work. No, we must be cunning and clever operatives, questioning all our assumptions, ready to read all the clues. We must be ready to see what is to be seen; ready to follow the trail wherever it leads. We must acquire the humility of Our Lady who knew that "the hungry he has given every good thing, while the rich he has sent empty away."

We must be true to our questions, but not question like outsiders, like bureaucrats with no real interest in their subject, or terrorists striving only to enforce their intolerance. When we confess our helplessness and drop the pretense that we already know the answer, that is when "the one who is among [us]" comes out of the shadows and makes himself known. "His mercy is from age to age on those who fear him." Yes, fear him, but not like the agents sent down from Jerusalem; rather like Mary whose lowliness he has regarded.

Fourth Sunday of Advent: God's game plan

"Let it be done to me as you say."

God has big plans for us, as today's gospel and Old Testament readings show. This is disarming because it shows that God is ever ready to turn the tables on us and pull the rug out from under us. God knows that if he is not careful with us, we'll begin to treat him like a difficult child or an aged and stubborn grandparent. That is, we will begin to humor God, or ignore him, or, in a fit of pique, tell him his place and what's best for him. And God, being God, will have none of that. So God upsets all our fine ideas about how things are supposed to be.

This is what King David discovered. After making a

success of himself as a general, he sat down and decided it would be good to do something for God just to show his gratitude. So he talked it over with Nathan, his advisor. Today Nathan might be called a media man or a campaign strategist. "Nathan," he said, "I think it's about time that we show God how much we appreciate his help in winning all these battles. Let's build a temple, a really fine one, so God will have a worthy place in which to dwell." But God told Nathan in a dream, "Tell that nice young man that he shall not build a house for me. I do all the building around here. Indeed, I will build him a house." Meaning, of course, not a dwelling-place, but a dynasty.

Perhaps David's intention was sincere. On the other hand, perhaps he just wanted to enhance his prestige. In any case, he was not to build God's temple; that would remain for Solomon, his son and successor. But the important thing is, God got his way. God indeed built a house for David, a long line of descendants which we reckon continues right up till Jesus. David was gracious about it, as one learns in reading the verses which continue where our first reading leaves off. But then, he didn't have much choice. God will be God. And David accepts that. David lets God be in charge.

And so does Mary. When the angel comes to visit her she doesn't give him a fight. She doesn't insist on her own way. She doesn't even question the extraordinary thing that is proposed to her. Unlike most of us, she is docile and transparent to the purposes of God. We are not transparent; we are opaque. We always see a shortcut, a more convenient arrangement, a less costly plan, and an easier road. Not Mary. Like David, she too is willing to let God be in charge. She is able to let God be the host.

This is something so difficult for us. Many of us are full of generosity, but sometimes it is a subtle form of pride. I have known people who would do anything for you. By the same token, they wouldn't let you do a thing for them. This reduces the possibilities to a rather one-sided relationship. The fact is, such people are afraid of becoming indebted, afraid of losing control. They always want to have their hand on the rip cord and know where the eject button is.

And we treat God the same way. We want to control him, appease him, keep him at arm's length. We sometimes let our natural goodness become an instrument of control to limit God's power over us. In a polite way we say to God, "There, I've kept your commandments, so do me the favor of leaving me alone. Just have a seat over there, entertain yourself, and be quiet until I am ready for you." But God tells us where to go, and refuses to be treated like a child, so that we end up wrestling with him like Jacob or arguing with him like Job.

That was not the way of David, who was gracious enough to lay aside his plans in order to receive God's hospitality. Nor was that the way of Mary, who was so gracious as to declare wholeheartedly and without hesitation, "I am the maidservant of the Lord. Let it be done to me as you say." Nor was it the way of Jesus, who received the hospitality of Mary, the sister of Lazarus; who permitted Mary Magdalen to wash his feet with her tears; who told his Father in the garden, "Not my will but yours be done"; who stretched out his arms on the cross; and who at last rejoiced to let the Father raise him from the dead.

The point is we must let God be in charge of our lives. We must accept the gracious hospitality, and what Julian of Norwich calls "the courtesy" of God. We must let God be our host. Christ knows this to be such a difficult thing that he arranged the eucharist to be our main form of worship, so that out of the sheer repetition of our doing this Sunday after Sunday, and day in and day out, perhaps at last we will give in. It is in this vein that George Herbert voices the human hesitation in his finest poem with the line:

> Love bade me welcome: yet my soul drew back
> guilty of dust and sinne.

To which the Lord, referring to the eucharist, answers and the soul at last submits:

> You must sit down, sayes Love, and taste my meat:
> So I did sit and eat.

CHRISTMAS

Christmas: Out of darkness, light

"Darkness . . . did not overcome it."

Christmas, like the event it celebrates, begins at night, in deep midnight. Darkness is the starting point. Indeed, in the northern hemisphere we are in the dark end of the year. The earth has turned its face from the sun, and we have just marked the winter solstice — the shortest day, the longest night. Night and darkness become emblems of our situation, our condition.

The night is cold and full of fear, as well we know. The night holds terrors. Darkness is the mask for misdeeds, and death lurks in the shadows. The gloom is partly relieved by the power of our technology to produce artificial light nearly everywhere. But there are still places we dare not venture after dark, and the occasional blackout is enough to remind us how frail is our grip on civilization.

Yet it is our darkness of spirit, our darkness of mood, and the darker side of our nature which is most troubling to us. It is the moral blackout, the cold night of unconcern, the gray specter of sin which haunts us. For we discover that the darkness is within as well as without. Our failures, our selfishness, our weakness have compounded our darkness by making us blind men and women, who wander under a starless sky, lost and without light.

To us Isaiah says, "The people that walked in darkness have seen a great light; and upon those who dwelt in the land of gloom a light has shone." Around us, as to those shepherds huddled against the cold, does the glory of the Lord shine. Because into the darkness of our world, into the darkness of our souls a tiny light appears. "This day in David's city a savior has been born to you."

That light, which appeared first in the eyes of the little baby born in Bethlehem, grew in brightness and outshone every light that ever was lit. That light is the assurance of real love and sure hope and lasting peace and eternal salvation. "For the darkness did not overcome it." That light was the grace of God appearing in our world to cast out darkness. For it is a "great and mighty wonder": Darkness, which seems so strong and so encompassing, is really weak. Even the smallest candle drives it out. But Jesus Christ is no little candle. He is the light of all the world, "the true light that enlightens everyone."

Let us be glad in him. Let us rejoice in his light. Let us gather to him and go to Bethlehem, drawn by the radiance coming from that stable. Let us know that it was for us that he came, even for us benighted sinners, for us who have been blundering around in the dark so very long. For he is the morning star and the sun of righteousness. Christ our light and our Lord.

Holy Family: Where grace grows

"The Lord bless you from Zion: may you see the prosperity of Jerusalem all the days of your life."

It is good that we celebrate this feast. It makes us think about something, and pray about something which is right under our noses and which colors and shapes the very meaning of Christmas: our families. We look at the crib today and we notice that the Son of God was born into a human family. This is perfectly obvious, but at the same time very telling. It tells us that the humanity of God is real. Christ entered into the fullness of our experience with all its joys and sorrows, all its stresses and strains. He did not merely pretend to be human. He did not inhabit a human body and animate it like a puppet. Rather, "by the power of the Holy Spirit he was born of the virgin Mary, and became man." And he did it within a human family.

That says something about God and about the "historical facts" of the life of Jesus of Nazareth, as far as they can be determined. At the same time it says something about us. It lifts us up and gives us heart. Today when families are under tremendous pressure and intense scrutiny, when we hear more than we would like about abused children and the tragic results of family problems, it is heartening to remember that God entrusted his own Son to human parents. Moreover, he made it so that the family of Nazareth, a poor family, was the place where the child Jesus would learn in his humanity the texture of human love, the sound and the smell of it, the sight and the touch of it.

This is the kind of thing we want to renew at Christmas. We want to repair and redouble our family ties. We want to recommit ourselves to the best values. We want to believe that such love, such grace is possible even in our families. And let us understand that "family" is a rich and a wide term. Let us think big enough to include every kind of family in our prayers today: families where there is a single parent, families where children are troubled. Let us include families some of whose members are separated by great distances — physically or emotionally, or who are separated this Christmas by death. Let us pray for those who are in the twilight of their life, who feast this day mostly on memories. Let us lift up to God families which are struggling or in pain. Let us see them too as places where the Christ child is born and real love is shared.

Finally, let us take a lesson from today's gospel. Every family needs to be related to the great family of all God's children. We go to the Mass today as the Holy Family went to the temple, to offer back to God what God has given us. Spiritually, let us all walk in the offertory procession today, bearing in our hands the sacrifice of our hearts. Let us place in the chalice our parents, our children, our brothers and sisters, all who are connected to us in the circle of family or friendship. Let us ask forgiveness. Let us offer peace. Let us give thanks.

"The Lord bless you from Zion: may you see the prosperity of Jerusalem all the days of your life."

World Day of Prayer for Peace: He is our peace

"I will hear what God proclaims; the LORD—for he proclaims peace to his people, and to his faithful ones."

It was Pope Paul VI, of saintly memory, who proposed that January first be set aside as a world day of prayer for peace. Those of a certain age can recollect the vagaries of the recent liturgical history of January first. It used to be called the Feast of the Circumcision. Perhaps because this evoked rather an Old Testament ambience, January first for a short while came to be the Feast of the Holy Name, and then to be called by the rather prosaic title, "The Octave Day of Christmas." Octaves don't mean much to anyone other than musicians, so that had little appeal. In the definitive calendar reform following Vatican II, January first became "The Solemnity of Mary, Mother of God." Liturgists hastened to assure us that this was the most ancient Marian feast, and the earliest name for this day in the liturgy at Rome.

Pope Paul VI was on to something when he asked us all to pray for peace on this day, and authorized a votive Mass to be said as an option. Of all the ways to mark this day in our calendar, this one makes the most sense. New Year's always means a new beginning and the rekindling of hope. Many make some kind of resolutions for the new year. (Whether they live up to them or not is another matter.) But the chance for a new beginning by the marking of a break in the rhythm of things fills the natural need to start over, to wipe the slate clean, to be freed of past mistakes, to aim higher for the future.

As we look at the world on the eve of a new year, perhaps we are tempted to cynicism. Perhaps we are apt to believe that this poor old, weary old, cold and grimy world is slipping backwards rather than forwards. There is never a lack of evidence for that. A browse through the newspaper or the year-end round-up in the magazines will confirm it. But, though we may overlook it, there has been good and hopeful news too. So it is a mixed bag. Taken as a whole the evidence is inconclusive, and the viewpoint will either be optimistic or pessimistic according as one's temperament, experience and outlook lead. But the World Day of Prayer for Peace is not meant to be a year-end news wrap-up. We gather at liturgy to hear the word of God, to pray and to receive the Prince of Peace in the sacrament of the altar. The divine diagnosis goes a whole lot deeper than the summaries of journalists. The Bible and the teaching Church want us to see that the symptoms of our malady are very deep indeed. Our struggles with peace and our failure to achieve it go way back. The diagnosis is: sin, original and actual. We inherit some and we add our own. But the diagnosis indicates a remedy.

To celebrate a World Day of Prayer for Peace is an act of faith. Were it not an act of faith, did it not require some faith-filled outlook on the world and the human condition, then it would be no more than a well-meaning but futile gesture, a *beau geste* against the cold and dark of the last night in December. But it is certainly more than that because it seems that what we do at liturgy — the prayers we say, the sacrament we share — is more than we can know or say. Peace must be built up every day, yet it is not a human scheme and not the sum of human efforts. Like the recovering alcoholic we must first admit that we are powerless over our condition. We must accept that peace is a work of grace in the first place. It is not that work for peace and struggles on behalf of justice are

14

optional. They are demanded by the gospel. It is rather that at root our view is essentially spiritual and depends on faith.

Christ is our peace, Christ alone. He has reconciled us to God. He brings us together. His will is that "all should be one." His work is the gathering of the scattered children of God. He paid the price on the cross, dying for our sins and the sins of the world. He invites us to live on in his love and keep the commandments, the greatest of which are love of God and love of neighbor.

Let us take to heart the words of the psalmist: "I will hear what God proclaims; the Lord — for he proclaims peace to his people, and to his faithful ones."

Suggested readings: Is 9:1-3, 5-6 [831.1]; Eph 2:13-18 [900.2]; Jn 15:9-12 [834.1].

Epiphany: God-learnedness

"They prostrated themselves and did him homage."

The world into which Jesus was born was quite unlike our own, and again just like our own. It was a world full of danger, a world full of Herods. That is, a world where government is looked to for assistance, but cannot always be relied on. A world of manipulation, as in "Go get detailed information about the child." A world full of lies, as in "Report your findings to me so that I may go and offer him homage too." A world full of envy and murder, as in what was to happen to the Holy Innocents.

Then as now, Jesus himself was the object of curiosity as much as sincere interest. It is hard to guess at the initial motivation of the Magi, though it seems certain that we would regard their beliefs as naive and superstitious. Yet they were open-minded and willing to take a chance. And finding the child, they were ready to do more; "they prostrated themselves and did him homage. They opened their coffers and presented him with gifts of gold, frankincense and myrrh." They put their money where their mouths were, something that you and I don't always do.

These are ways in which the world into which Jesus was born is like ours. But it also seems different in important ways. His world was full of omens. There were stars to be followed and dreams to be dreamt. The stars and the dreams revealed wisdom and important guidance. This is true not only for the Magi but for Saint Joseph as well. In the gospel passages which were read in the days leading up to Christmas, Joseph, like his Old Testament namesake, was shown to be quite a dreamer.

We don't go much by dreams today. We prefer the hard data of science and mathematics. For us, information isn't trustworthy unless it can be expressed digitally, unless it can be crunched in a computer. Every day we can do faster and vaster calculations, but we seem to be no closer to the real meaning of things. The alternative for us is not to be gulled by horoscopes and tea leaves; we must remain children of our generation. Still, we may have lost what stars and dreams really mean in the context of this gospel — a belief and trust in something besides ourselves, something transcendent, something not available to empirical investigation, something that cannot be proved but only believed.

Perhaps this is the real gift of the Magi, not to the Christ child but to us: they help us to recover faith in the transcendent. They show us that even wise men and women can get beyond skepticism and cynicism. They show us that sophistication and learning has unexpected dimensions. The old and formal Dutch word for "theology" is *godgeleerdheid* or literally, "God-learnedness." God-learnedness: the Magi stand not only for the respectability of that, but also for its very possibility.

The Epiphany is an invitation to God-learnedness. It means to say that if we are willing to listen and see, the Lord Jesus will show himself. If we are prepared to go on a journey, if we are ready to set out in search of him, he will leave clues in our way and footprints along our path. If we will but go to Bethlehem, that most unlikely place, we will be surprised — but never disappointed. For "he shall have pity on the lowly and the poor; the lives of the poor he shall save."

May the light of Christ, rising in glory, guide us to his heavenly kingdom.

Baptism of the Lord: Checking the compass

"You are my beloved . . . On you my favor rests."

Today we stand at a crossroads, at a turning of the path. For if our liturgy and Church year can be likened to a journey of discipleship, where we walk down the days in company with Jesus, then we have come to a bend in the road. It is because according to our liturgical reckoning of time, Christmas ends today and the "Season of the Year" is about to begin. And that is like coming to the crest of a hill and seeing the vista of the lands that lie aback and ahead. Cresting the hill affords time to catch one's breath and enjoy the view. It is also the time for compass reading and having a glance at the map, to see if reality matches the chart.

Looking back, we see that on the first Sunday of Advent we heard the prophet cry, "O that you would rend the heavens and come down." And today in the gospel of the Lord's baptism we heard that the heaven was indeed rent, and Jesus manifested as Son of God and anointed with the Spirit. We get a bearing in the other direction, too. Today the first song of the "servant of God" is read out of the book of Isaiah. Scanning the horizon, we see it will be read again on Monday of Holy Week, just as we are coming to the brink of another hill, the mountain of Calvary.

This is what I mean about checking the map against the landscape, these correspondences between where we have been, are now, and are headed. Today's feast, therefore, is a recapitulation and a preview. It sums up Christmas and gives a glimpse of the life and ministry of Jesus which is to unfold in the gospels of the next weeks and months.

But what does the baptism of the Lord itself mean? It is not the same as our baptism. It is not that Jesus became a Catholic today. It means something else. Perhaps we can think of it as the passing of the baton in a relay race. John the Baptist is finishing his sprint. Although he appears in the opening pages of the New Testament, he is really the last of the Old Testament prophets. Jesus' submission to John's baptism of repentance marks the transition from the old covenant to the new, from law to gospel, from prophet to Christ. It marks the beginning of the gun lap, the final phase of the race.

This is made clear in the outcome of the baptism. St. Mark says, "Immediately on coming out of the water [Jesus] saw. . . the Spirit descending on him like a dove. Then a voice came from the heavens, 'You are my beloved Son. On you my favor rests.' " In the liturgy of the Eastern Churches, Catholic and Orthodox, this feast is called *tes photas*, "the lights," or the "holy theophany," that is, the "holy manifestation of God." Moreover the East sees the baptism of Jesus as merely the first of many theophanies, many showings of God. The ministry of Jesus is begun at his baptism in the Jordan. His life and miracles, his death and resurrection are but further demonstrations of the kingdom, the new life, the power of God to make all things new and all people one.

The power of the Lord's baptism, the Holy Theophany, is that it intersects our lives still. It has been woven into the fabric of human existence. It is right there on the map and on the horizon if only we have the eyes to see it. It happens in this way: God continues to be manifest when we, like Jesus, take the form of a servant; when we, like him who broke not the bruised reed nor quenched the smoldering wick, hold back the angry fist of violence. God is shown when we, like Jesus, open the eyes of those blinded by prejudice and hate; when we bring out those confined in the prisons of compulsion and addiction. God is revealed in the man and woman of any nation who fears God and acts uprightly. God is made credible when you and I, like Jesus, go about doing good works and healing those in the grip of the devil.

All of this is possible in our lives. For the Father says of us also, "You are my beloved . . . on you my favor rests." He has anointed us for mission and ministry. We journey with Jesus. He goes before us into Galilee. He will be transfigured before us; and he will minister to us. So look out over the landscape. Take the food of wayfarers to strengthen you for the journey. Hear the words which a famous Christian pilgrim, John Bunyan, puts in the mouth of one of his characters, "Mr. Valiant for Truth":

Who would true valor see
Let him come hither;
One here will constant be,
Come wind, come weather.
There's no discouragement,
Shall make him once relent,
His first avowed intent,
To be a pilgrim.

LENT

Ash Wednesday: The acceptable time

*"For our sakes God made him who did not know sin
to be sin, so that in him we might become
the very holiness of God."*

Lent begins so dramatically — ashes smeared on
foreheads. It is such a stark and primitive gesture that it
seems to be almost prehistoric. This is the stuff of
anthropology, cutting right through all the sophistication
of our education, our civilization, our late twentieth-cen-
tury technology. It drags us back to our ancestors and
shows that for as far as we have come, we are not so far
from them — not so far from the cavemen, nor from
Adam and Eve.

Ashes remind us where we came from and where we're
going. "Remember that you are dust and to dust you shall
return." There is the unvarnished truth of it all. Death,
the great leveler, will come to claim us, every one of us.
And us, we are sinners. What is more, we know it, little as
we like to say it. We are sinners who are going to die. We
bear the mark of Cain on our brows; death is in our blood
and in our genes. Rarely do we face reality with such brutal candor. But today the Church grabs us by the scruff of
the neck and sticks our face in it. Ashes are smeared on
our foreheads to show us once again what the score is.

The ashes are free but come with a warning. Today's
gospel is like the government health warning on the
cigarette pack: "Ashes are dangerous to your health." And
so they are. Smeared ashes are so vivid a symbol that we
could be fooled into thinking that by receiving them we

had really done something when, in fact, we will have done just nothing. The gospel brings us up short. These ashes mean nothing — unless something happens inside. "Do not behave like the hypocrites," says Jesus. "They change the appearance of their faces so that others may see they are fasting. I assure you, they are already repaid." God is impossible and his Ash Wednesday is impossible. Am I to take the ashes or not? Am I to do something, or nothing? God can't decide which it is to be.

God has decided all right. God wants it all. God wants our hearts, souls and bodies this Lent. Ash Wednesday is a day when God demands sovereignty over us in a forceful and compelling way. Ash Wednesday is a day of truth, of humiliation and penance. It is a day for unburdening the soul and purging the body. It is a day for laying aside all pretense, for dethroning "King Ego" and his courtiers "me, myself and I." It is a day for kneeling and confessing that there is one God, one Lord, and one alone is holy.

But is Ash Wednesday confirms God's sovereignty, it likewise celebrates our liberation. It has the power to break the grip of the ordinary and thus free us enough to make a new beginning. That is its value. It is such a fracture of routine and self-expectation that it creates space. It unshackles us from our illusions and compulsions; spreads wide the fault line of our insecurity. It creates an opening and makes us free for a moment.

While we are free we must run to Jesus. Let us kneel before him and confess our sins. Let us be disciples and walk with him this Lent. Go into the desert with him, fasting and praying. Wrestle with Satan and discover the strength God will give you. Let sin be sin so that "in [Christ] we might become the very holiness of God." Pray, fast and give alms. Do not be afraid. Do not shrink back. As you see, we are all in this together. "Now is the acceptable time. Now is the day of salvation."

First Sunday of Lent:
Noah made 'em all play ball!

*"You are now saved by a baptismal bath
which corresponds to this exactly."*

There is a vigorous and delightful spiritual which goes like this:

A way, way back in the ages dark,
Ole man Noah built a sea-goin' ark.
Ole man Noah had his nervous spells
When he had to listen to the animals' yells,
But when anythin' was doin'
He was there with bells:
He was a grand ole sailor!

Ole man Noah knew a thing or two.
Because he knew a thing or two
He thought he knew it all.
Some say he was an "also-ran",
But he was th' original sailor man.
Ole man Noah knew a thing or two;
He made 'em all play ball!

Today's readings evoke all sorts of memories of bible history lessons, children's picture books depicting the ark perched on the top of Mount Ararat, and taking the family pets out on the boat, and songs like the one foregoing. "Ole man Noah . . . he was a grand ole man!" He certainly was, and it's too bad the whole story is not read of his adventures in the ark: he, his family, and his floating zoo. But that story is well known, and enough is read out to bring back those memories.

Noah is memorable not so much for his nautical derring-do as for his faith, and because god made a covenant with him. Noah represents God's wanting to give human folks another chance, a new start. God made a covenant with him, promising that the earth would never again be destroyed by flood. In token of which God set the rainbow in the sky, or so the story goes. The deeper message here, as always, is quite simply God's love for people, expressed concretely in the story of one man's family long ago and far away, but it might just as easily be now and be your family.

Yet St. Peter sees even more in the yarn, as we hear in today's epistle. The waters of the flood are a foreshadowing of baptism, "which make an end to sin, and a new beginning of goodness." As God brought Noah and his family safely out of the waters of the flood, so God has brought us from death to life through the waters of baptism. It is good to remember our baptism, to bless ourselves with the holy water, to celebrate the *Asperges* at the beginning of Mass, to feel the water again, to know once more what Christ did for us through those life-giving waters.

The Church reads about Noah on the first Sunday of Lent to remind us that on the first Sunday of Easter we will stand together before the altar and renew our baptismal vows. Lent is for getting in shape to do that. Lent is for living up to our baptism. Lent is for limbering up — by prayer, fasting and almsgiving — for the race that we row in the ark.

"Ole man Noah . . . some say he was an also-ran / He was th' original sailor man." May we not be "also-rans" this Lent, but winners — like Noah, and Peter and Jesus. Let's get both oars in the water and all pull together.

Second Sunday of Lent:
Love was his meaning

"[God] . . . did not spare his own Son
but handed him over for the sake of us all."

Many are scandalized by the story of Abraham and Isaac. They are troubled by the idea that God would demand a human sacrifice, that God could be so capricious as to test Abraham's faith in such a cruel way, asking him to sacrifice his son. Commentators tell us that there is a biting irony in this passage, that it is in fact a polemic against the human sacrifice practiced by Israel's pagan neighbors. God's intervention in the nick of time is a way of dramatizing the evil of such a sacrifice.

At the same time it is true that the Bible uses this story as a means of exalting Abraham's obedience and his faith. Since the two elements are so closely interwoven, the sacrifice of the child remains a stumbling block for us. If we back away and take in the larger context we see that all of the stories in the patriarchal history, which begins in chapter thirteen of Genesis, are about the promise made to Abraham and the circuitous path of its fulfillment. In this context it makes even less sense for God to demand the life of Abraham's son, for God would, in effect, be thwarting his own plan. Yet the episode would still have meaning for Abraham as a lesson in how God must be trusted absolutely. Abraham cannot see too far forward. None of this makes sense to him. The fulfillment of the promise depends on God above all, and Abraham must learn, as all of us must, that he can't save himself; only God can. God's ways are not our ways.

Even then we cannot put behind us the troubling notion of the sacrifice of the well-loved son; St. Paul brings it up again in the second reading. He speaks about God "who did not spare his own Son, but handed him over for the sake of us all." So we cannot keep this thought safely locked in the Old Testament where it may freely be passed over as primitive and developmental. Clearly it plays a part in Paul's own understanding of the cross and the salvation won on the cross.

Surely Paul uses this image because of its familiarity to Christians of Jewish background, to whom the story of Abraham and Isaac is well known. Moreover, we see from their writings that the apostles and Church Fathers constantly make all sorts of connections between the old covenant and the new. For them the two existed side by side as prophecy and fulfillment. It would be fairer to say that the Old Testament retains its validity; it is meaningful in its own right. But for us who are Christians the story continues and includes Christ. Christ is the center. St. Mark's gospel shows us the crucified and risen Christ as the center of meaning, the interpreter of human existence, the salvation of the world.

In this light, the attempted sacrifice of Isaac by Abraham is no more heinous (far less, in fact) than the criminal death of God's Son on the cross. *That* is the real stumbling block. The cross was a scandal for the first generation of believers and remains so for us. Yet the crucifix has been deeply graven in our imagination and has taken root in the symbolic imagination of our culture. Taken casually, as it often is, it has lost its power to shock. We wear it in gold around our necks; we inscribe it on every pew end and holy water sprinkler; we bless ourselves with it countless times with scarcely a thought. But when we stop to think, when we sit in the church or in our room and contemplate it, when we meditate on the individual scenes of the passion as we do when we make the Stations of the Cross — only then do we begin to collect the real horror of it, the real cost of it, the real power in it, the real hope from it.

It is because the cross is so scandalous, so insupportable from the human standpoint, that Jesus must prepare his disciples for it by first showing them his glory. In the words of the spiritual, Jesus wants them to "keep their eyes on the prize." The mountain of transfiguration anticipates the mountain of Calvary, and yet the two are so closely connected that the meaning of each can hardly be separated. The message is neatly summarized in the old jingle: No cross, no crown. It may be a jingle but it is deeply true. It is gospel: No cross, no crown.

Jesus bids us lift our eyes toward him. We see him in glory revealed to the disciples on the mountain. We contemplate his glory as he now is, seated at the right hand of the Father. But we also see that his hands still bear the marks of the nails, and his side the wound opened by the soldier's lance. He is the crucified and risen one.

Take to heart these words of the 14th-century English mystic, Julian of Norwich, who saw with dazzling clarity both the suffering and the glory of the cross and the meaning of the words, "[God] . . . did not spare his own Son, but handed him over for the sake of us all":

> [God] suffers because it is his will and goodness to raise us even higher in bliss. In exchange for the little we have to suffer here, we shall have the supreme and unending knowledge of God which we should never have without it. The sharper our suffering with him on his cross, the greater our glory with him in his kingdom. (*Revelations of Divine Love*, ch. 21)

Third Sunday of Lent:
The measure of the world

"For God's folly is wiser than men,
and his weakness more powerful than men."

"Christ (crucified) is the power of God and the wisdom of God." Those words are a razor which cleaves through all human activity and all human meaning. Believing and living them is the measure of a Christian believer. The

26

cross is the emblem of the faith. Many wear it around their necks, bless themselves with it, or expect to find it on the spire of the church or on its stationery. But when it gets down to seeing what the cross really means and what it really costs, many falter.

No surprise in that. St. Paul clearly expects it. The cross, he says, is a stumbling block (literally, a scandal) to Jews and an absurdity to Greeks. He means no one can make sense of it, neither in the terms of Old Testament religion nor human philosophy. Everyone has trouble with it because it goes so much against the grain. Here we are already at the heart of the matter. The cross turns our values upside down. The cross stands for everything we don't believe in, try to avoid and hold in contempt. For we humans believe in success, but the cross means failure. We believe in winning; the cross means finishing dead last. We believe that what you see is what you get; the cross looks like nothing at all. We believe in grabbing what you can; the cross means having a nail driven through that hand.

The cross of Christ proclaims that death is not the end, and life is more than material success. The cross means that there comes a time when we have to walk the plank and believe that someone is going to hold us up when we hit the water. The cross strips away every illusion, all the niceties, all the masks, all the pretense, all the courtesy. The cross is brutal. It forces a choice. Can I believe it, despite all the evidence to the contrary, despite all my instincts to turn away and forget?

That's how it looks from the outside, and those who remain outside will probably always be frozen there, poised at the brink, wondering, hoping for a sign, dying to be convinced, and dying of the uncertainty. But "to those who are called" it is "the power of God and the wisdom of God." It cannot be proved, only lived. It is only when we have been dragged kicking and screaming, only when we are so desperate that there is nowhere else to turn, only when some faithful and courageous Christian has shown us by simple words or, more likely, a brave death — only then are we ready to believe and trust.

And then finally we see for the first time how the foolish gospel of the impossible God really does make sense. Then we begin to grasp what Cardinal Newman meant when he said that "the cross of Christ was the measure of the world." Then signs and proofs become unnecessary. Then all that is needed is proclamation: "For God's folly is wiser than men, and his weakness more powerful than men."

Fourth Sunday of Lent: Gospel love

"Yes, God so loved the world that he gave
his only Son, that whoever believes in him
may not die but may have eternal life."

These are famous words. This verse is known far and wide: John 3:16. Its citation is even held up on placards at sporting events. Evangelical Protestants in particular like to proclaim it, and with good reason. It is sometimes called the little gospel because it epitomizes the good news in one single declaration. And what a rich and fruitful sentence it is.

Think about it. "God so *loved* the world." The good news is that the Father loves us. God wills to be gracious. Salvation is established and offered to us and to all for "God so loved *the world*." The love of God is wide open, comes with no strings, is not hemmed in by political tests nor ethnic or racial quotas. It is not "a limited time offer," but remains eternally valid. God "gave his *only* Son." God's self-gift, the Son's self-emptying is the proof of this love. "And there is salvation in no one else, for there is no other name under heaven given among men by which we must be saved." Moreover, it is clear from the context that this "sending" means not simply the incarnation but the crucifixion as well, for "so must the Son of Man be *lifted up.*" Indeed, it is the whole paschal mystery that is meant here. "God *so* loved the world," signifying the fact of redemption but also its cost — the cross. Finally, the sentence encompasses both an invitation and a promise. The invitation is to faith in the Son, to "whoever *believes in him.*" The promise is rescue from death and the gift of eternal life, since "whoever believes in him *may not die but may have eternal life.*"

In the face of so joyful and positive a message, who could fail to be moved? Whose hopes or wishes would not be buoyed up in hearing such a promise? Who could turn away without finding strength and comfort from words such as these? And yet we know that many are not convinced. Many find in these words no balm, but briars and bitter herbs. If we look deeper we understand that the announcement of the good news with its offer of salvation always provokes a crisis. It brings its own difficulties, or rather lays bare the impossibilities that beset us: the sin of the world which entangles us, our pride, our shame and the stubbornness of our hearts. Naturally we suspect "good news." Nothing good comes for free, we say. Where's the catch, the hook, the hidden cost? And what is love after all? We are, some of us, not so sure we believe in that anymore. We've seen too much, been too often hurt, not least by God. So don't say "God so loved the world."

Then again it may be we are glad God loves us, but are not so sure God's loving the world is a good idea. The world doesn't deserve it. Like Jonah we are jealous of the Ninevites. We feel slighted somehow by God's interest in those we regard as our inferiors. We feel that if God's love is not exclusive it can't be worth very much, and if it's that cheap we are not interested. We sense clearly enough the horizontal dimension of God's love, the outstretched arms of the cross, and we shrink back. Or maybe it is just the opposite. The love of God is too precious and we cannot pay. The cross is beyond our means even should we mortgage it, especially then. We are defeated by an overmastering sadness. We see what would make us really happy but we lack the courage to enterprise it. We are downhearted and forgetful.

We forget that Jesus says, "And I, when I am lifted up from the earth, will draw all to myself." In the end John 3:16 remains good news because it is God's word. And the one who was lifted up will indeed draw us to himself. For the love of God is stronger than our doubt, stronger than our pride, stronger than our sin, and stronger than death. The good news is that all our objections are met and answered in these gospel words, for they are more than words. They are sacrament; they do what they say. They make the love of God visible and credible. All we must do is accept. "This is not your own doing, it is God's gift." Such is the testimony of those who have seen, who have tasted, who have lived, the testimony of John and of Paul, the testimony of those who gather in the name of Jesus Christ: to break the bread and pour the cup, to proclaim and deepen their faith in all that is eternal, to hear and to say again:

> Yes, God so loved the world that he gave his only Son, that whoever believes in him may not die but may have eternal life.

Fifth Sunday of Lent: Sight for sore eyes

"Some Greeks . . . approached Philip . . . and put this request to him: 'Sir, we should like to see Jesus.' "

These lines from the beginning of today's gospel are oddly touching. They refer to a request made by some Gentile disciples. That is, they refer to an historical event in the ministry of Jesus, but also to a theological event — the opening of the kingdom to the Gentiles, to the *goyim*, to non-Jews. And yet they have a still wider application and a deeper force. "We should like to see Jesus" is such a touching request precisely because we recognize it written in our own hearts and issuing from our own lips.

"We should like to see Jesus" are the words that sum up our deepest longing and our truest aspiration. When we are quiet enough to listen to our hearts, honest enough to recognize our poverty and our failure, when we are courageous enough to hold out our hands to God, this is the cry on our lips: "We should like to see Jesus." "We should like to see Jesus" in the midst of our pain and confusion; see him at the heart of all our relationships; see him in the workplace and in the midst of our family where we live out our lives day by day.

"We should like to see Jesus," not because he is famous and we will be magnified by contact with his celebrity. We seek him because he is our savior. We want to see Jesus because we've heard he is a prophet and a holy man. We want to see Jesus because we are more than curious; we want to see him because we hope he will heal us, touch us, help us, give us peace. And the Jesus we find is always more than the one we sought. He is always more than we hoped, more than we dreamed, and more than we bargained for. So it was for those Greek disciples. Their request is relayed up the chain of command from Philip to Andrew and then to Jesus. And Jesus gives them their answer, but likely not the one they are expecting. He seems to go off on a tangent and talk about something entirely different. "Unless the grain of wheat falls to the earth and dies, it remains just a grain of wheat. But if it dies, it produces much fruit." What kind of answer is that? And what kind of riddle?

"We should like to see Jesus." When we don't see him it is because we are distracted or looking elsewhere. We miss him because our sins have blinded us, because our attention was on ourselves, or because we have turned our back and lost him. But he looks for us and finds us. Moreover, the evangelist tells us where we must look. Jesus says, "I — once I am lifted up from earth — will draw all to myself." But what can this mean? Here is the answer. If we want to see Jesus we must behold him on the cross. If we want to know Jesus we must know him in his passion, death and resurrection. If we want to love Jesus we must imitate him in his sacrifice. If we want to live with Jesus we must first be ready to die with him.

And still, "We should like to see Jesus." He is our hope. "If anyone would serve me, let him follow me; where I am, there will my servant be." This is the answer that Jesus gives to those who seek him. What we make of this answer is in our discretion. It is up to us. But he says, "Anyone who serves me the Father will honor."

Let us go to see Jesus.

Passion (Palm) Sunday: Light in darkness; the way in doubt

"The spirit is willing but nature is weak."

We encounter a fundamental ambivalence in today's liturgy. Hence its twin titles — Passion Sunday, Palm Sunday — and, since we prefer the bright side, the popularity of the latter. This gap is most obvious in the dramatic shift from the palm procession with its shouts of "Hosanna" to the passion with its shrieks of "Crucify him." The ambiguity is very deep, rooted as it is in the abyss of the human heart. It rends the fabric of human life as decisively as the curtain in the temple sanctuary was torn from top to bottom in two. We may name it the battle of light with darkness, the struggle of good and evil, the war between virtue and sin, the contention of flesh and spirit, the mystery of death and resurrection, but it is here that the salvation of the world is played out.

Life is full of ambiguity, full of false starts and mixed signals, and we keep surprising ourselves. Are we fundamentally wicked or good? Why does our unyielding self-interest poison even our most noble aspirations, our most generous gestures? Why do we unfailingly make tragedy out of comedy and persist in hurting even those closest to us — especially them? Is there really freedom for us or is it merely the ghost of a wish? The same may be asked about truth. Why do we persist stubbornly in falsehood when we are trying desperately to be honest — honest with ourselves and others, honest about the world and honest to God? Why is the truth so awful to face? Why do we hide it from ourselves? Why does the world in one moment feel welcoming, beautiful and friendly, and in the next hostile, cold and ugly? Is God for us, or against?

Jesus himself was no stranger to this ambiguity. It is played out in his life and especially in his passion and death. He enters Jerusalem to the cheers of the crowd and leaves to their jeers and spitting. He announces his betrayal "as they were at table eating." But isn't the meal supposed to be a sacrament, a moment of intimacy and trust, of companionship and solidarity? Shortly, in a twisted sign, a token of human affection will become the perverse instrument of his arrest. "And when he came, [Judas] went up to him at once, and said, 'Master!' And he kissed him. And they laid hands on him and seized him." The kiss leads to betrayal; the embrace to arrest.

Then in the garden Jesus experiences the full weight of what is upon him. He knows most bitterly the pain and anxiety, the fear and ambiguity all feel. He knows there is an easy way out for him, but that it will cost his very soul. And he is tempted to take it. Jesus, who is truly man as the creeds teach us, "fell on the ground and prayed that, if it were possible, the hour might pass from him. And he said, 'Abba, Father, all things are possible to thee; remove this cup from me; yet not what I will, but what thou wilt.' "

The disciples too are torn apart by the same ambiguity. The disciples fell asleep in the garden for "the spirit is willing, but nature is weak." And at the arrest they ran away. Peter, always so straightforward and open-hearted, wants to stand by Jesus. He follows and says to Jesus, "Even though they all fall away, I will not." But in the high priest's courtyard, in hostile territory, Peter "began to invoke a curse on himself and to swear, 'I do not know this man of whom you speak,' " Peter is confronted with his impossibilities and faces them honestly. He "remembered how Jesus had said to him, 'Before the cock crows twice, you will deny me three times.' And he broke down and wept."

In a final irony, Jesus, who ate with sinners and thereby earned the jealousy of the good, is finally done to death as a criminal. "And with him they crucified two robbers, one on his right and one on his left." For it is Barabbas, a man "who had committed murder in the insurrection," who is preferred to the innocent Jesus. Pilate, the cool administrator, who is well able to see what is going on, chooses the way that is politically expedient, and the result is judicial murder.

Yet in all of this the will of God is accomplished. Even in our crookedness and ambiguity, even when meaning well we do ill, God is able to bring out life from death, grace from sin, truth from lies. Karl Rahner has written:

> The world and its history is the terrifying, sublime, death-and-immolation liturgy which God celebrates unto himself by the agency of mankind. The whole length and breadth of this monstrous history, full of superficiality, stupidity, insufficiency, and hatred on the one side, and silent dedication, faithfulness unto death, joy and sorrow on the other side, constitutes the liturgy of the world, and the liturgy of the Son on his cross is its culmination.

Rahner continues:

> And if the secret essence of the world's history, at once stupefying and stimulating, wells up from the depths of [the Christian's] existence and overflows the land of his heart, he is not surprised that thus he experiences the grace of the world. Judgment when refused, blissful future when accepted, this grace permeates history, and in the cross of Jesus it has already reached the point where it can no longer be defeated. (*How to receive a sacrament and mean it*)

It is this grace that we celebrate today and in the week to come. It is this grace which makes the cross light in darkness, the way in doubt.

Holy Thursday, The Lord's Supper Mass: The death of the Lord

"Every time, then, you eat this bread and drink this cup, you proclaim the death of the Lord until he comes!"

The last supper of Jesus with his disciples is overshadowed by the cross. It is a sacrificial meal. All three readings show us this in evoking the "tradition" of the Lord's Pasch, its forerunner in the Jewish Passover and its sacramental extension in the eucharist.

[The lamb] shall be slaughtered during the evening twilight. They shall take some of its blood and apply it to the two door posts and the lintel.

Every time, then, that you eat this bread and drink this cup, you proclaim the death of the Lord until he comes!

Jesus realized that the hour had come for him to pass from this world to the Father.

This Mass is overshadowed by the cross. These readings concern death and the sacrifice of Christ. We may forget this as we celebrate the liturgy this night, as we walk around the church in procession, our senses full of the beauty of lilies and silk vestments, and with the fragrance of incense clinging to us. We may forget this sacrificial dimension, not only because of the beauty of this evening's liturgy, but also because of its comfortable familiarity. The Mass is for Catholics our principal service. It is the main thing (and too often the only thing) that we do when we gather for prayer. It is the touchstone of our shared experience of worship. It is what makes tonight so typical and tomorrow, when there is no Mass, so odd.

The liturgy of the Evening Mass of the Lord's Supper re-confirms our experience. We do what we are accustomed to do; what we have been taught to do; what, as it were, we naturally and normally do. We do it in remembrance of Jesus and in obedience to his command. We do it as something received from the Lord, handed on to us by our parents as they likewise received it, and so on in the "faith which comes to us from the apostles." It is like a smooth stone lying in a stream bed. Washed by the water of the centuries it has become smooth and beautiful. But it is a stone which, when we see it turned over, retains its sharp edges. It is a stone which cuts and gashes. Beneath the smooth ritual, the familiar and well-practiced gestures, is life and death, raw and bloody. "Every time, then, that you eat this bread and drink this cup, you proclaim the death of the Lord until he comes!"

What Jesus says and does over bread and wine would make little difference and have no effect were it not for the cross which follows. The Last Supper is in anticipation of Calvary, as the Mass is in anticipation of the heavenly banquet. If the Lord's body were not stretched out on the cross, then he could not say, "This is my body *which is for you*." If his blood were not poured out on the cross, then the cup words "the *new covenant in my blood*" would be nonsense. If the Mass is not the sacrament of a sacrifice, and if we do not feel the enormity of it tonight, then all we ever do in church is make believe and waste our time.

Christ offered himself for us as the Lamb of God, as sacrifice of the new covenant, as the servant who poured out his life in service. This is the Passover of the Lord. This is the meal which makes a new pilgrim people. This is the grain which, buried in the earth and dying, gives life. And we take part in it. Tonight we make our communion with him in it.

The Flemish poet Guido Gezelle captures the sense of the eucharistic sacrifice of Jesus in which we share. At the end of his poem *Panem de coelo* come these lines:

> O God, who slain, much like the grain,
> fell before the flail;
> bestow that bread on me, I pray, now
> and again,
> ere my heart must fail!

> O God, who, like a noble wheat
> mildly milled, were flung
> into the furnace, to the cross, where,
> baked by heat,
> brown as bread you hung;

> O young ambrosial Manna, mighty
> manly victual, give
> me strength to go one day, when dying,
> God almighty,
> where you ever live!

Good Friday: Love was his meaning

"In this is love, not that we loved God, but that he loved us, and sent his Son to be the expiation for our sins."

These lines from St. John's first epistle are a key with which we may unlock the meaning of this day and the meaning of our every human struggle and striving. "In this is love." Look at the crucifix. "In this is love." Behold the image of the Son of God nailed to the cross. "In this is love." Consider his head crowned with thorns, his body torn and bleeding. "In this is love."

But this doesn't look like love. This is not what you or I think of when we think of love. Love is supposed to be wonderful and beautiful, all romance and roses. And

37

there is none of that in this. "There was no comeliness in him. He was a man of sorrows and acquainted with grief." Yet "in this is love." The word which St. John has for love is the Greek word *agape*. He means by it a love which is completely gratuitous, and in which the hope that love will be returned is not a condition for loving. Usually *agape* is translated as charity, but that may be misleading. *Agape* is not the extra change we throw into the poor box. It is not even the substantial pledge we make to our favorite worthy cause.

If you want to know the definition of *agape*-love just look at the cross. "In this is love." And there is nothing in our experience quite like this love, no analogy to spring from, nothing to compare with it. "Not that *we* loved God . . ." It is almost beyond our ken, out of this world. It is more than one can say or know. "Not that we loved God, but that *he* loved us." And in loving us enabled us to love. God loved us, and in loving us made us lovable and lovely. But has it made a difference? Is there any sign that men and women are any different, let alone any better, than they were two thousand Good Fridays ago? There is the question.

And here is the answer: "(God) loved us and sent his Son to be the expiation for our sins." Are we any better? That question is a trap. It distracts us from the cross where we ought to be looking, and instead draws us inward to ourselves. But the answer is surely not to be found in ourselves; it is there nailed to the cross. "God sent his Son to be the expiation for our sins."

Perhaps that is why it is so hard to look at the cross. Our sins and the sins of the world are nailed to it, and when we see it, we see them. Take a good look. See if you cannot discern there all the brutality, all the torture, all the violation of human rights that fills each day's newspaper and each night's broadcast. Look upon the crucified and see if you cannot recognize, not only the heinous and gross crimes of humanity, but also the petty egotism, the small, stupid foolishness which appeared trivial but ended in tragedy. Can you not find a place for your sin up there? "God sent his Son to be the expiation," the atonement, the sacrifice which takes away the sins of the world. And that is why the cross is gospel, is good news, and not just another statistic from the police blotter, one more atrocity for Amnesty International to catalog.

The meaning of the cross is that our sins are taken away. The meaning of the cross is that death is not the last word. The meaning of the cross is that we don't have to go on crucifying one another. Because of the cross there is another choice, another option, a new possibility. The meaning of the cross is that God loves us in spite of all, and with a love deeper than anything we could imagine. The meaning of the cross is that "in this is love."

On the night of May 8th, in the year 1373, in the city of Norwich, England, a young woman lay dying. In her anguish there was given to her a vision of Jesus crucified. The full measure of his sufferings became very vivid, became her strength in the depths of affliction. In the event she recovered and spent the rest of her life as an anchoress, a hermit, telling people of what she had experienced and how it had changed her. Mother Julian, as she came to be called, wrote of her vision. She cherished and preserved the memory of it, so that other souls in their anguish could find meaning and comfort in the passion of Christ. She wrote:

> You would know our Lord's meaning . . . ? . . . Love was his meaning. Who showed it you? Love. Why . . . ? Love . . . and I saw . . . that before ever he made us, God loved us; and that his love has never slackened, nor ever shall. . . . In this love our life is everlasting. (*Revelations of Divine Love*, ch. 86)

"In this is love, not that we loved God but that he loved us, and sent his Son to be the expiation for our sins."

EASTER

Easter: Seeing with the heart

"Then the disciple who had arrived first at
the tomb went in. He saw and believed."

The gospel passage for Easter morning proclaims the heart of our faith. It tells us far more than we may imagine, and at the same time less. First, notice that today's gospel does not describe the resurrection, an event terribly difficult for us to imagine. The New Testament writers certainly believed and taught that Jesus rose from the dead. They surely also understood his resurrection to be not just a simple resuscitation, but a transformation of an altogether different order. What the resurrection actually is is a crucial question for us. Our faith is based on it, and we would naturally like to have some distinct idea about it. We would like to be able to imagine what risen life is really like. But the scriptures are silent. The actual resurrection of Christ is nowhere described in either the gospels or the New Testament letters.

What we hear proclaimed today is not an account of the resurrection but the report of an empty tomb, and that is something distinctly different. If you already believe, the empty tomb makes sense. It confirms the story, since it would be awfully hard to convince people Jesus was risen if his body still lay in a famous tomb. But the empty tomb is susceptible of more than one interpretation, for it can also suggest that Jesus' body was stolen and hidden for propaganda purposes. That this is not too wicked a notion to be suggested in a meditation on Easter morning is proved by the gospel itself. Clearly Mary Magdalen thinks the body has been stolen. She says,

40

"The Lord has been taken from the tomb! We don't know where they have put him!"

But here is something interesting for us. One of the central characters, Mary Magdalen, who is reported in all the gospels as first at the scene, is not immediately convinced of the resurrection. The same is true of Peter. He is not first at the tomb; Mary, the other women and the Beloved Disciple all precede him, but as leader of the Twelve he is surely a more central character. And what does he conclude? The evangelist tells us Peter saw — he saw the empty tomb, he saw the grave cloths. The evangelist does not tell us he believed. The evangelist is deliberately silent, for Peter is undeclared. He is careful, even reluctant, and not without reason. Too much is at stake.

Peter will become a believer and so will Mary, for the gospel relates more than the empty tomb. What seems more important to the evangelists than the empty tomb are the appearances. The risen Lord appears to Mary and Peter, to the two disciples on the road to Emmaus, to the disciples on the shore of Lake Tiberias, and to the gathered apostles in the upper room. The first Christians are witnesses, not to the mysterious event within the tomb at the moment of resurrection, but to its result, to him who has been raised. What convinces them is the risen Christ whom they encounter, who speaks and eats with them, who opens the scriptures to their understanding, who calls to mind all that he had said, who bids Thomas place his hand in his side. The empty tomb is not unimportant, but it is background and context. The authentic and unmistakable presence of the risen Christ is what really does it. But let us return to the scene at the tomb.

The empty tomb and the grave cloths are an invitation. They are not proof in a scientific or coercive way, but are signs, and signs can be read by those who understand. Both Mary and Peter see, but do not believe. Who is it that both sees and believes? It is the other disciple. And who is he? Though his name is not spoken, this "other" disciple is the disciple whom Jesus loved, the "Beloved Disciple." And this too is a sign. See for yourself what it

41

means. The Beloved Disciple sees what Mary and Peter see, but the Beloved Disciple sees *and believes*. This is because love can see beneath what is apparent to merely bodily eyes. Love can see the meaning. Love can read the heart. Love is sensible of the inner reality. Love perceives spiritual truth. Love is persuaded by evidence unseen.

Let us imitate the Beloved Disciple. Let us draw near to Christ with faith and devotion. Let us see with our hearts. Let love guide our way. Let what the mystical author of *The Cloud of Unknowing* calls "a dart of longing love" take us to the target. Let us understand that all the evidence we need is already in our possession. The evidence is written on our hearts. It is the name Jesus. His word is the declaration of God's love. His sacrament is the earnest of eternal life, of true resurrection. We behold the empty tomb. In love let us recognize that what seems empty is really full, that he who is departed is truly present, that what is promised has been fulfilled, that what is pledged is already given. We too are witnesses to the risen Christ. In the words of the apostle: "After all, you have died! Your life is hidden now with Christ in God. When Christ our life appears, then you shall appear with him in glory."

===

Second Sunday of Easter: Doubts disappear in the abyss of love

"Peace be with you. . . . Put your hand into my side. Do not persist in your unbelief, but believe!"

Poor old Thomas! In one way I pity him, and in another I'm glad of him. I feel sorry for him because he got a "bum rap." Fame has saddled him with the nickname "Doubting Thomas" — forever! And that is so unfair. I'm sure there were many other qualities he would have preferred to be known by. For instance, tradition tells us he was the apostle who brought Christianity to Kerala, in the south of India. There he is known as Mar Thoma, a term of affection and respect. Instead Thomas seems destined to be remembered for the incident related in today's gospel: "Doubting Thomas." Yet there is ever a good side to that, at least for us. Thomas makes the apostles seem more real, more human, more like you and me. Thomas makes me feel better when I have doubts. Thomas helps us to be honest and unashamed in confronting God with our hesitations and fears.

Let's be honest, all of us have moments when we're not so sure, when we lose our self-confidence, when we think about God, "Maybe I've just dreamed him and invented all of this." There are moments when we wonder why God hates us, why our life is not as charmed or easy as someone else's we know. Perhaps we've wondered why God has taken a loved one away from us, or have been jealous of God's favor to another. Perhaps there is something about the Church that is difficult for us to reckon with; some teaching that is hard to accept; some priest who has hurt us; some contradiction between what is taught and what is actually lived. These things make believing difficult. Perhaps, like Thomas, we even wonder about the resurrection. We'd love to believe in it, but it all seems rather vague. And when it comes down to my own death, can I take the chance?

At such moments Thomas is a comfort to us, because he represents, as it were, an acknowledgment from God's side and a recognition on God's part that believing is no easy task. It is demanding. It is risky and foolish. Believing in Christ come back from the dead is quite a venture. And building a life around that naked conviction demands unparalleled courage, because we have precious little hard evidence that it is true. Thomas appeals to us because he is a skeptic and a cynic. He will not be gulled. He's no one's fool, the perfect man of today, an empiricist who must be shown. "Unless I see and touch . . . I'll never believe." Thomas wants proof. He finds a personal encounter.

In a sense his temptation, the temptation of the skeptic and the doubter, is to go on the defensive, to take the position against belief, to dare anyone to prove the contrary. See, twice already in this gospel passage it is noted that the disciples were gathered but the *doors were locked*. This was out of fear, fear that they would get the same as Jesus, that they would be crucified too. But I think the locked doors are emblematic of something else, something deep within the human personality. Profoundly hurt, disappointed, disillusioned, scared by the horrific and sudden demise of their master, the one they had left their jobs for, whom for three years they had tramped around Judea and Galilee after, the disciples display a quite normal reaction. They withdraw, go into hiding, pull back and nurse their wounds.

The temptation is really the temptation to give up. It is the temptation, not to doubt any new evidence which may be offered now at the critical moment, but to doubt the evidence they already possess, the evidence of their experience. They actually have in their possession all the evidence they need; it lives for them in their memory — the knowledge of Jesus first hand, his stories, his miracles, their words with him, feelings for him, hopes in him. This is what Thomas is doubting. This is the door that has slammed shut. His question is: Was it all real? Can I trust my experience? Can I live by it? Was I deluded? Am I mad? That is Thomas' problem. And the enthusiasm of his colleagues is just salt in his wounds. They have moved on, been converted, made the passage. He is still stuck, left behind; therefore, left out.

But Thomas encounters the risen Christ. Suddenly what he already knew is validated. What was at risk is assured. What was imperiled is rescued. What was falling apart is put back together. Christ is alive and life can go on. The point is, without facing doubt and uncertainty we, like Thomas, remain immature and vulnerable. If we do not learn to break down the locked door and trust another, our life will wither away.

Jesus invites you and me to unlock the closed doors of our hearts. Put away fear and take the hand he extends to you. Believe what you have seen. Trust your experience with him. Know that he is more real than anyone or anything you can know. Place your hand in his side and let all your doubts and fears disappear in the abyss of his love.

Third Sunday of Easter: The faith that comes from the apostles

"Everything written about me in the law of Moses and the prophets and psalms had to be fulfilled. . . . You are my witnesses of this."

To die: to sleep;
To sleep: perchance to dream: ay, there's the rub;
For in that sleep of death what dreams may come,
When we have shuffled off this mortal coil,
Must give us pause.

Hamlet's uncertainty about what lies beyond death strikes a chord in all of us. All of us have our moments, moments of wondering, moments of hesitation or uncertainty about what is to come after. Perhaps they are not even doubts, just the restlessness of not knowing.

Our faith is a comfort to us, but even our faith answers few of our many questions. Beyond the fundamental question, "Is there anything at all?", there are many others. What can it be like? Will I recognize people? Is there conversation, and eating and touching? And if there is some kind of life after, mustn't it be so strange, so disembodied as to be . . . unhuman? What we can glean from the gospel is helpful but incomplete. There is so much more to know and understand. But we can be thankful for what we have been given.

Today's gospel records an appearance of Jesus to the disciples after his resurrection. St. Luke is clear that this is a real encounter and not clairvoyance, not a delusion or a hallucination. Jesus meets his disciples, speaks and even eats with them. They recognize him because he is recognizable. He is the same, but different. He has a physical presence, but it is not limited in the usual way.

What we can know and say about the resurrection is this: The disciples proclaimed it as real and not as a symbol in the sense of a thing devoid of substance. It is far more than that Jesus' ideals, his spirit, what he stood for lives on. The disciples proclaim that the Jesus they knew was indeed raised from the dead in the body. He is the same, and he is different. He has a body, but it is glorified. He has been transformed. There is continuity with what they knew and remembered; but there is a dimensional difference; there is something new now, something not previously experienced about him.

The resurrection also means a change in the disciples. They too are the same but different. They are full of courage, full of joy, full of peace. When Jesus appears, "peace" is his greeting and his gift. And that gift has clearly had its impact.

The last thing about all this is that there is no proof, at least not to any acceptable scientific standard. What there is is testimony and the invitation to trust and believe. "You are witnesses of this," he tells them. The resurrection is believed because faith in it has been passed on from one generation to the next. "The faith that comes to us from the apostles" is how we say it in the first Eucharistic prayer.

So we must make a leap and be willing to take a risk. We must dare to stake our life on it and become witnesses to what we have not seen. But we can witness to his risen power within us. We can testify that already we have experienced peace. Already we have touched him. Already we have eaten in his presence. Already found the hope and the courage and the love.

Christ is alive and makes intercession for us. Christ is alive and so we can live.

Fourth Sunday of Easter:
Watching over Israel

"I know my sheep and my sheep know me."

The image of Jesus as the Good Shepherd remains a powerful and touching one. This is true even though the green pastures have long since been paved over with asphalt, wool has largely been replaced by synthetics, and lanolin is to be obtained only from plastic bottles.

Objections to the pastoral import of this passage may more likely be heard along the lines, not of cultural irrelevance, but that sheep are perhaps the dumbest of animals and to compare them with human beings today is patronizing in the extreme. However that may be, and despite the undoubted technical advances of the twentieth century, years as a priest persuade me that we humans will still give sheep a good run in the race for the foolishness prize.

The real power of the image of the Good Shepherd lies in the intimacy that it suggests between our Lord and us. We may have moved away from the farm generations ago, but we all still yearn for intimacy, for closeness, for someone to care about us and take care of us. In the gospel this is expressed in Jesus' words, "I know my sheep and mine know me." This knowledge is the knowledge of love, the knowledge of experience. It is like the way you know your spouse or your children, from having watched and listened to them, from having lived with them.

The closeness of family ties is further suggested in today's epistle when St. John says, "See what love the Father has bestowed on us in letting us be called children of God! Yet that is what we are." And that is the way God, our heavenly Father, wants to relate to us. That is the kind of knowledge and love that is expressed in the image of the Good Shepherd. The Good Shepherd loves us and so watches over us. Because he watches over us he knows us. His knowledge and love are inseparable.

There are two kinds of watching, you know. There is surveillance, the vigilance of the FBI or a police stakeout or sting. This watching is meant to produce evidence. Its aim is to catch the thief red-handed. But that is not how God watches us. God is not looking to trap us, though many may have been taught to feel that way. And there is also that watching which a parent does over a sick child; the admiration with which one beholds one's beloved; the pride with which we review a parade or watch our children graduate from school. It is in this second way that God watches us.

This is confirmed by many texts in scripture. Most remarkable of all is the beautiful story of the call of Nathaniel in the first chapter of St. John's gospel. Jesus addresses Nathaniel as a "true Israelite." Nathaniel is startled by that greeting and asks, "Rabbi, how do you know me?" And Jesus answers him, "Before Philip called you, while you were sitting under the fig tree, I saw you." That is how the Good Shepherd watches over us — not with morbid curiosity but with sincere interest, not hoping to catch us out, but hoping to buoy us up, not as a warden but as a dear parent and the lover of our soul.

Come to him then, to the guardian and shepherd of your soul. Invite him in to sup with you. Follow him who will not lead you astray, but will bring you safe to the kingdom, to live there with him for ever.

Fifth Sunday of Easter:
Loving God as our own child

"Live on in me, as I do in you."

As a child I was never very good with plants. Few of the marigold seeds I planted ever sprouted, and those that did were soon savaged by small animals foraging in my garden. When I was growing up, carrots were still sold with their greens attached. We'd put the tops in a dish of water to get them to root. But I could never wait. Invariably, in my curiosity, I'd pick them to pieces leaf by leaf. Agricultural lessons were lost on me, so I hesitate to say much about this wonderful story of the vine and the branches. Square-foot gardening, victory gardening or any other kind of gardening is just not in my line. But there is still something appealing here even for those of us who lack a green thumb. Behind the details of vine cultivation lies a touching lesson. Jesus is saying to us that we need one another. We need him, and he needs us.

That in itself is startling because we think of God as needing no one, as being by definition totally self-sufficient. How could God need us? Perhaps in the way that we need someone we love. God needs us because he loves us. When you give your heart to someone you need them. No one can live without a heart, and when you have entrusted your heart to another, you depend on them to keep you alive and to make you happy by the return of their love. So it is with God and ourselves. The Father cares for us, reaches out to us, waits for us. Jesus wants us to be with him, wants us to need him, wants us to love him. When we realize that, we begin to see how true are the words of Jesus: "I am the vine and you are the branches." He is speaking of the way in which he and we must live together and grow closer.

Every Spring we celebrate Mothers' Day and Fathers' Day. These celebrations disclose to us the mystery of the kind of mutual dependence Jesus proposes. Children need their parents. They need them for food and clothing, for protection and care. Above all they need their moms and dads to love them and smile on them, just as their parents need their children to return their love and surprise them every day with their discoveries of growing up. And this love needs to be expressed.

It is just this way that we need Jesus. We need him in our daily prayer and our weekly worship. We need his holy bread of the eucharist to make us strong: strong in faith and strong in love. St. John tells us today that "we must love in deed and truth and not merely talk about it." That needs practice in all of us, and we can accomplish it only with God's help, only if we are grafted to the true vine. But we must discover our need of Jesus precisely as adults and as parents. There is a Dutch poet (Gerard Cornelis van het Reve*) who proposes the crazy idea that we must love God as our own child. This is because he takes the love of parents for their children as a generous and sacrificial love, a love that, when it is true, asks nothing and gives everything, a truly godly love. I think this poet has seen something true.

Could it be that Jesus wishes you to love him as your own child, to love him as Mary loves him? Could it be that he meets you today, perhaps even after an absence, and invites you to abide in him, invites you to bear much fruit? He says, "Live on in me, as I do in you. . . . If you live in me, and my words stay part of you, you may ask what you will — it will be done for you." I take these words from today's psalm as God's blessing on those who would endeavor to love him in such a way: "They who seek the Lord will praise him: 'May your hearts be ever merry!' "

*Cf. Huub Oosterhuis, *Poems, Prayers & Songs*, p. 122.

Sixth Sunday of Easter: Love's commands

"You are my friends if you do what I command you."

For a long time I misunderstood this verse. To me it sounded like *quid pro quo*: "You scratch my back and I'll scratch yours"; "I'll let you play with my football if you make me quarterback." There was something about it that didn't ring true. It made Jesus seem manipulative and self-interested like everyone else. And, since I have as much trouble keeping the commandments as everyone else, it seemed to me uncertain that I could ever qualify to be Jesus' friend. Not too encouraging, this verse, if this is what it means.

Happily it doesn't. The problem is in reading and understanding the verse as if it were "If you do what I command you, then I'll be your friend, says the Lord." That sounds like something one would expect to hear and often have heard, but it is not in fact what Jesus says. Jesus' love for us is not conditional but absolute. Jesus does not love us if we are good or when we are good. Jesus loves us — period. His love makes us good.

The correctness of this interpretation is proved by the epistle, which says, "Not that we loved God, but that he loved us and has sent his Son as the offering for our sins." And again in today's gospel when Jesus says, "It was not you who chose me, it was I who chose you to go and bear fruit." So it is Jesus who makes friends with us. It is his invitation, his initiative. Then it is up to us whether or not to respond. "You are my friends if you do what I command you" really means "You return my friendship by keeping my command. You show your love and loyalty, you demonstrate your fidelity when you keep my command."

But isn't all this talk of commandments far from the way friends speak to each other? Surely friends do not command one another? They ask. At times they may even plead, but command? Never! So there is still a problem.

Again, not so. In the gospel, the Greek word for "friend" has the same root as the word which describes the love of parents for their children. Everyone knows and accepts that parents must give commands if they really love their children. "Don't touch, that's hot!" "Stay in the shallow end of the pool!" "Be nice to your sister!" "Give mommy a kiss!" Take this last. By straight syntax it may sound like a cold command, an order, but the context shows it to be an invitation. Such are love's commands.

Love and commandments are not mutually exclusive.

Sometimes they couldn't exist without one another. The commandments give definition to love. Without them love would be vague and meaningless. And love, as we see, is the commandment of Christ. "The commandment that I give you is this: that you love one another." And as he asks of us, so he demonstrates for us: "There is no greater love than this: to lay down one's life for one's friends." Let us be proud to be known as the friends of Jesus. Let us keep the command of the Lord and abide in his love.

Solemnity of the Ascension: Heaven, our home

"The Lord Jesus was taken up to heaven and took his seat at God's right hand."

The Ascension means that Christ has completed his work and is now the exalted Lord of the universe. The Ascension is an aspect of the Easter mystery. The Bible and the liturgy use a figure to convey this, the image of being seated in a place of honor. So in the psalm we have: "God mounts his throne with shouts of joy." And in the epistle: "It is like the strength he showed in raising Christ from the dead and seating him at his right hand in heaven." And in the Creed: "He ascended into heaven and is seated at the right hand of the Father."

The idea of the royal throne is alien to our American experience, as we have no king or queen. But the theme of the place of honor and authority is not at all strange. In business we know the chairman of the board who sits at the head of the table. In the law we have judges who hand down decisions from the bench. In the university professors are appointed to chairs in the various subjects. In the cathedral there is the *cathedra*, or bishop's chair, the seat he presides from. And we speak of the Holy *See* or seat, which refers to the chair of Peter, the papal office. You also know that when someone rings your doorbell the measure of how welcome they are is whether or not you invite them in to take a seat. And when someone important enters the room we instinctively rise from our seats out of respect.

The Ascension means that Jesus is God's well-loved Son. He is Lord and king, worthy of our worship. But it also means something for us. The Ascension reveals our destiny, hope and calling. In the opening prayer we prayed, "May we follow [Christ] into the new creation, for his ascension is our glory and our hope." And in the preface we hear, "Christ . . . has passed beyond our sight, not to abandon us but to be our hope . . . where he has gone, we hope to follow."

Jesus, in his Ascension, is showing us what to expect. Not only are we to rise from the dead, we are to go to heaven too. Heaven is our home. And we mustn't think of it as so awfully far away, as impossible, as never-never land. Heaven is where Jesus is. Heaven is here because the Lord does not leave us orphans, but is with us. Heaven is yet to come because he has gone to prepare a place for us. May he bring us safe to his kingdom, and shed his peaceful light on us.

Seventh Sunday of Easter: Consecrated for witness

"Consecrate them by means of truth."

Let us explore those words. "Consecrate" means to set aside for a sacred purpose; to place in the realm of the holy; to make holy. We use it of things: churches and chalices are consecrated. Bread and wine are consecrated to become the body and blood of Christ. But persons are also consecrated. Many bishops, priests and deacons have been ordained in our cathedrals. Even more babies have been baptized, children confirmed, and couples married in our churches. In this gospel Jesus prays that his disciples may be consecrated, that the Father might consecrate them. One can say that he prayed also for us in prospect, and so we have been consecrated.

"Consecrate them by means of truth." Remember Pilate's question, "What is truth?" Here Jesus gives an answer. "Your *word* is truth." What is this word? "The Word was made flesh and dwelt among us . . . and we have seen his glory, the glory of an only Son coming from the Father, full of grace and *truth*." The word is Jesus. And the truth is that God loves us and gave his Son for us. The truth is that the Son consecrated himself on the sacred altar of the cross for us. The truth is that in baptism we have already been consecrated to him, that is, claimed and set apart. The truth is that his word dwells in our hearts by the Holy Spirit, whom the Church awaits as the days of Pentecost draw to a close. The truth is that the word is already visible in our lives, but not perfectly.

One last point. Consecrated chalices are kept in safes and vaults to protect them from thieves. Not so the consecrated disciples of Jesus. We are consecrated, not to be locked away for safekeeping, but to bear witness to the truth, to bear witness to Jesus, to bear witness to God's love. May our Lord consecrate and hallow us. May we be his witnesses and faithful stewards of the riches of his love.

Pentecost: Locked in by fear; set free by peace

" 'Peace be with you,' he said again."

We think of Pentecost as an extraordinary episode long ago. We think of Pentecost only as tongues of fire and speaking in foreign languages. We think of it as a not-often-seen phenomenon. But the gospel describes Pentecost in more familiar terms. In this passage St. John shows us something we well know and experience often.

On Easter Sunday night the disciples are in hiding. "The disciples had locked the doors of the place where they were for fear of the Jews." They knew what had happened to Jesus. In John's unfolding of the story, Mary Magdalen has encountered the risen Lord in the garden, but the rest of the disciples have not. They do not yet know of Jesus' rising. All they know is he is dead, crucified on Friday noon. The rabbi they had been following is dead; all their hopes and dreams are dead. Now it is Sunday, and what is their fate? They may well presume that they are on a list, that people — police, death squads, Romans, Jews — are even now looking for them, wanting to make sure that this movement is stopped in its tracks, that its devotees are weeded out root and branch. Of course they are afraid. Why shouldn't they be? Withdrawing, locking the doors, that is the smart thing to do.

But Jesus visits them. Twice he greets them with the words, "Peace be with you." But there is more than words; there is encounter. He shows them his hands and his side. It is really he, and he is really present with them. So it is words and presence. Pentecost is an encounter. It is a meeting that makes a difference. It is a presence which transforms death to life. It is a gift of peace which banishes fear.

We have all had such experiences. Remember them. On a visit to London by myself during Holy Week, I was feeling very disconnected, very uncomfortable. All right, I was lonely. All the museums and churches, all the theater and music could not make up for the family and friends, the faith community I was missing at that intense time. On the night before Easter I received a phone call from a friend who would meet me for Easter dinner next day. That call was a gift of the Holy Spirit. It was salvation from a lonely holiday. It replaced fear with peace. And there was the time my father underwent dangerous surgery and the family waited at the hospital for some word from his doctor. When the news came through, but not just the news, the consoling presence of the surgeon still in his green scrubs telling us everything had gone well, that too was Pentecost and a gift of the Holy Spirit.

God's Spirit is given when we set one another free by a gift of compassion and presence. Pentecost happens when someone's visit unlocks the inner room of fear or loneliness, of dependency or compulsion where we have been hiding. The risen Lord is manifest when we hear the words "Peace be with you," and when they are reiterated until we finally believe them. We begin to believe them when a compassionate friend shows us his or her own wounded side and hands. Then we get the idea that even we may rise. Then the greeting of peace can get through our thick skulls and unbelieving hearts.

But there is one thing more. Notice that the episode does not end just with a gift of peace. A solitary contentment is not the purpose of Jesus' visit, though sometimes that may be the most we are capable of when we first feel his touch. Jesus brings a charge and a mission. "As the Father has sent me, so I send you." The disciples pass from being stuck to being send. They go from fear to mission. They leave the locked room and go out to proclaim the name. They bring his peace to the world.

This gospel episode has become a prayer said at every Mass, and not a bad prayer to make part of our personal devotion.

Lord Jesus Christ, you said to your apostles:
I leave you peace, my peace I give you.
Look not on our sins, but on the faith of your Church,
and grant us the peace and unity of your kingdom
where you live for ever and ever. Amen

Corpus Christi: The blood of the covenant

"I will take the cup of salvation,
and call on the name of the Lord."

The feast of the Body and Blood of Christ is meant to help us treasure the "wonderful sacrament" which Christ left us in the eucharist, a "memorial of [his] suffering and death," as well as a pledge of our future glory. Today's readings are arranged to help us meditate particularly on the blood of Christ, "the blood of the covenant, [which was] poured out on behalf of many." This is something which we are not apt to think about. We often think about the eucharist under the species of bread, the body of Christ. We rarely reflect on the eucharist under the species of the wine, the blood of Christ.

There may be many reasons for this; most of all because we are so used to receiving communion in one kind, receiving the host alone. We think of that as normal, and communion under both kinds as special. Whereas if we pay attention to the Last Supper we find the opposite is true. Receiving communion under the form of wine has become more frequent as a result of the liturgical renewal. This is a very good thing, but it will take time and effort to put it fully into practice.

There are, however, other reasons we do not think about the saving blood of Christ. Blood is frightening to us. How many times have you heard someone say that they faint at the sight of it? How many people shy away from being blood donors and potential life-savers because the thought of giving up their life blood is so scary for them? We fear blood because it may be dangerous, especially since we know it can be the medium for the transmission of HIV, hepatitis and other diseases. Moreover, the religious idea of blood connected to sacrifice is brutal and repugnant to us. It seems horrific, like the gory crime stories we read about in those terrible supermarket tabloids.

There are many reasons why we shy away from blood

and so do not see the rich spirituality of our Church's deep devotion to the blood of Christ. Today's scriptures try to show us that the blood of Christ, shed for us, makes us right with God. It washes away our sins. It is a perfect offering which never has to be repeated. It makes a new covenant between God and us.

In the first reading we heard how Moses sprinkled the blood of the sacrificial animals on the altar, representing God, and on the people, thus uniting the two. Just so, in the sacrifice of the new covenant, the blood of Jesus, the blood which he shed in his passion, the blood which flowed from the wounds in his hands and side, joins us to God our Father perfectly and forever. It atones for our sins. The word "atone" really is "at one." Through our communion in the body and blood of Christ we are at one with God.

This is the message and meaning of today's feast: The blood of Christ is the life of Christ given up for us. The blood of Christ is the love of Christ spent freely on us. The blood of Christ is his salvation freely poured out for us. You know, it is really the great Christian poets and hymn writers who see it and say it best. The 14th-century English mystic Richard Rolle wrote:

Jesus, love made thy tears to fall,
'Twas love that made thy blood to flow,
For love was scourged and smitten all,
For love thy life thou didst forgo.

And Charles Wesley, the great Methodist hymn writer, expressed it in these words:

O for a heart to praise my God,
A heart from sin set free,
A heart that always feels thy blood
So freely spilt for me.

May the blood of Christ save us from our sins and reconcile us to God. May the sacrament of Christ's body and blood, given as bread and wine, preserve us unto life everlasting.

SEASON OF THE YEAR

Second Sunday in Ordinary Time: Getting sex right

"Glorify God in your body."

St. Paul has some interesting things to say about sex in today's epistle. Evidently there was some funny business going on among the parishioners in Corinth and he has to help them get their perspective right. In a way it's comforting to know that even the earliest Christians, whom we tend to idealize, had their problems getting sex right and living up to the high demands of the Gospel. It may be instructive for us, then, to examine the line which Paul takes with them.

Essentially he wants them to see sex in an integral way. There was a religious outlook, a contemporary philosophy called Gnosticism. The Gnostics were an elite who felt they had an insider's knowledge about how things really are. They were the bright young things of their day, the trendy set, the "in" crowd. They were convinced that they knew better, or at least, that they knew something which regular folks didn't know. And this private knowledge, this sophistication, assured them salvation. Moreover, they were dualists. They regarded matter as inferior to spiritual and psychic reality. Thus they would not be held responsible for their bodily actions, since in their view that sort of thing doesn't count for very much. "Anything goes" might have been their motto. You know how sometimes a very small child who breaks something will claim that he didn't break it, his hand did; that is just how the Gnostics argued. They had a disconnected view of life. According to them they were not immoral; it was their drives, their bodily urges that were acting up. And we know that it's not worth paying much attention to them, or so they thought.

It is often said that the Church is too preoccupied with sex, that it is always negative about it and just wants to make people feel guilty. It seems to me that everybody is already preoccupied with sex. Everything has come to acquire sexual connotations, right down to which toothpaste you buy or which car you drive. Moreover, the evidence shows that religious people have no monopoly on guilt. The "liberated" people of today are keeping a small growth industry booming in the form of advice books, "call-in" experts, and the new priesthood of analysis. By contrast, St. Paul has something quite positive and constructive to offer here. Paul is holding out for sexual responsibility, sexual integrity. He is saying that how we behave really does matter; that our mind, our spirit and our body have to work together. Paul values sexual expression; his idea is that it is inherently meaningful. To treat it casually is to distort it and to demean oneself. Thus "the body is not for immorality; it is for the Lord. . . ."

There is a "gnostic" climate today. Take an example. The "Playboy Philosophy" poses as a kind of insider's knowledge which smirks at the conventional morality. All it really is is good old-fashioned American capitalism applied to sex. For Hugh Hefner (and daughter Christy) sex is one more commodity to be traded, to be bought and sold. It is marketed as essential to the ensemble of the successful man or woman: a fast car, the right Scotch, the latest stereo gear and an attractive partner — all to be traded in when something (or someone) better comes along. But "gnosticism" does not have to take such a pretentious or silly form. Playboy is only an obvious instance of a pervasive attitude. The consumer society, greed, the drive to compete, the privatization of every area of family life and ethical concern, all these contribute to the climate.

All our temptations to sexual sin — not our sexual feelings themselves, but the temptations to misuse sex — are

60

temptations to a fragmented view of reality. It is to see one good and exclude other goods. It is to make the partial whole. It is to make what is felt as urgent to seem eternal, which it is not. The temptation to sexual misconduct, beyond its physical manifestations, has this meaning: it is to hide our identity from ourselves and to make ourselves the center of the universe. Of course we do not often recognize this in those passionate moments or when our relationships have gotten into deep water. The charm of the serpent which bewitches us still is an all too ready willingness to deceive ourselves and believe that things are other than as they are. But the gospel strips away illusions and demands reality. When Adam and Eve discovered that they were naked it was only their illusions about one another and about themselves which had disappeared.

The gospel replaces illusions with hopes, and self-deception with true sight. We are temples of the Holy Spirit, arrayed in holy attire. Our bodies are valued, bought at the price of God's Son and given back to us for freedom. And we are meant to "glorify God in (our) body." This we do in our work and in our play; in the marriage bed and at the altar; in the intimacy of the family and in the arena of the world. May the Lord keep us holy — body, soul and spirit — and bring us safe to his heavenly kingdom.

Third Sunday of Ordinary Time: A new start

"This is the time of fulfillment. The reign of God is at hand! Reform your lives and believe in the good news!"

The preaching of Jesus is simple and direct. Yet each of these sentences says a lot.

First: "This is the time of fulfillment." The preaching of Jesus is a heralding. It marks a new beginning. It creates a window of opportunity, a door through which we may walk to encounter God. Our human experience shows this to be necessary. How often have each of us had the desire to do some good, the urge to patch up a difference, to make a new beginning, but failed because we lacked the entrée. What we needed was a "time out" in which we could be sure that new initiatives would be welcome. We needed the encouragement to make a go, to take a chance. This is what Jesus affords us in proclaiming a time of fulfillment.

Every religion keeps a calendar filled with many or few sacred days, high times in which the god may be approached. The incarnation of Christ and his preaching of good news means every day is available. The invitation is an open one. God has made himself approachable by becoming one of us. There are, to be sure, special days and high feasts, days of grace and opportunity, but every day and every moment is radically open to grace. A way we used to say this was that the death and resurrection of Christ threw open the gates of heaven. And it is just so.

"The reign of God is at hand!" This is the central theme in all Jesus' preaching and teaching. This is what his miracles and many healings mean. The kingdom is coming and is here. God is establishing his rule over human hearts. All who accept the Son become friends of the Father. And in so doing they are set right with God. Their sins are forgiven and they inherit eternal life. The reign of God involves the individual believer, but also all of creation. The world as we know it is being transformed into the world we hope for. The announcement that the reign of God is at hand is linked to the first statement, "This is the time of fulfillment." It means that salvation is available; grace is near.

"Reform your lives. . . ." This means more than meets the eye. The Greek is *metanoiete*, which literally means change your minds, change your thinking. Therefore the reform which Jesus preaches goes beyond simple moral conformity. It is much more than merely towing the line or keeping to a certain standard of behavior. This is a critical point because it is often misunderstood by critics of the faith and by believers as well. It may be that religion serves a certain social purpose in restraining the more outrageous and dangerous human instincts, but this is not its main purpose or validity. Whatever moral values the gospel carries with it, and we know that they are demanding indeed, they spring from an inner vision, a new grip on reality, a new way of seeing oneself, the world and God. Mature Christian virtue is the fruit of a new perception and a new relationship, not mere external conformity to a code.

The traditional word for this is conversion. In the practical sphere it means that I strive to be good not out of fear of punishment, at least not mainly, but in order to be faithful to the love and forgiveness, the peace and joy which faith in Christ has given me. Again, we used to distinguish between imperfect contrition (attrition) which springs from mixed motives, and perfect contrition, which is prompted wholly by the love of God. Jesus is inviting us to be perfect, but not as a work or project of ours, rather because through him we know the love of God and are buoyed up and transformed by it.

". . . Believe in the good news." This is the complement of conversion, that sea change in thinking and acting to which we are bidden. And what is the good news? It is the whole gospel. It is everything that Jesus says and does right up to and including his passion, death and resurrection. Jesus and his message are inseparable. We cannot, as some think, take the best of his noble ideas without taking him. Christianity without discipleship is counterfeit. Therefore we see in St. Mark, just after this great statement of theme, the call of the disciples: "Come after me; I will make you fishers of men."

Here St. Mark tells us a startling thing. "They immediately abandoned their nets and became his followers. [. . .] They abandoned their father Zebedee . . . and went off in his company." There is the demonstration of it, the consequence of his call. Christ is demanding. He will not settle for less than our complete faith and devotion. But all he really needs to see is some small step in his direction, some reaching of our hand toward him, even some twitching of our finger, some hopeful look of our sad eyes. That is enough; he'll do the rest.

He calls: "This is the time of fulfillment. The reign of God is at hand! Reform your lives and believe in the good news." With the psalmist, let us just say, "Teach me your ways, O Lord."

═══════════════════════════════════════

Fourth Sunday of Ordinary Time: Who's in charge here?

"A completely new teaching in a spirit of authority!"

Today's readings raise the problem of authority in the Church. And when we think about the "problem of authority" we see that it is really a knot of problems, a series of thorny issues which fit together.

On the one hand the problem of authority is the natural resistance everyone has to being told what to do. We like to think of ourselves and do it our own way, especially today. This is an age of individualism, and everyone, at least in the industrial West, has a heightened sense of their personal worth, their destiny, their sovereignty over their own lives. But it has not always been so. There was a time, a very long time, when individual rights were held more in balance with the rights of the community. Individual freedom of choice was subordinated to a sense of solidarity with the group, a strong feeling of belonging to and contributing to something greater than oneself. Tension is experienced today between personal fulfillment, or at least what is perceived as personal fulfillment, and the good of the majority. It is a tension felt in every sphere of life, secular as well as religious, and it contributes to the problem of authority.

But there are other authority problems. There is the problem of those who don't wish to think for themselves at all. They do not want responsibility. Rather they want the complete assurance that they are right, that their choices are safe, that all risk of failure has been eliminated or narrowly restricted. This type of personality finds very attractive the lifestyle of cults and fundamentalist sects.

Then there is the problem of the abuse of authority, an old and familiar problem. Ordinarily there are mechanisms within society to deal with it. There are the checks and balances in our Constitution; the offices of consumer advocates and ombudsmen for minorities; review procedures for the use of force by the police; canonical safeguards for the rights of Christ's faithful, even of theologians. It is this problem, the abuse of authority, or the perception of its abuse, which is raised when the media show us an embassy being picketed, or a demonstration in front of City Hall — or a bishop's cathedral.

But there is also that problem which arises when authority is weak or non-existent. It may be that this is an authority problem not enough considered. It is this problem which the book of Deuteronomy is grappling with. Who is to lead God's people after Moses is gone? How is there to be continuity? How are we to maintain contact with our roots? The answer comes that God will send prophets. But this is not an adequate or convincing answer because it provokes in turn the further question: How are we to know whether these prophets are true or false? The Hebrew scriptures show there is no easy or foolproof way to tell a true prophet from a false one. It comes down to "By their fruits you will know them," and by that time it may be too late.

Then there is Jesus. St. Mark presents him as one who has authority and exercises it. The gospel shows that Jesus is not embarrassed by his authority, does not wear it uncomfortably, but uses it continually to demonstrate the kingdom of God. He preaches in the synagogue convincingly; he casts out unclean spirits. Our authority problems may be brought into focus if we look at Jesus. He shows us that authority is something necessary. Someone has to make decisions and put them into effect for the good of the community, whether that is the family, the parish, the diocese or the universal Church. Sometimes that is us; sometimes one set over us. Authority and power is neither the whole answer nor the whole problem. Nothing human would work without it, and a whole lot would work better if it were better used. So it is not a question either of abolishing authority or worshiping it. It is a question of using it rightly.

And above all, we must believe this: Christ still abides with his Church and governs it. This he does through the power of the Holy Spirit. That power is manifest in those appointed to govern the Church, but more and more we can recognize it in the life of every faithful Christian. For there is the power that comes from office, from a ministry given in the name of the Church for the building up of the Body. But there is also that power which comes from the wise use of the gifts God has given each of us.

Perhaps the most authoritative power anyone of us possesses is the authority that comes from true holiness. When we live lives of self-sacrificing love, of committed discipleship, of action for justice, then we have an authority no title can bestow. Our authority comes from Jesus, who set us free and made us whole. Our authority comes from the cross that we carry each day, and the faith that we bear in the power of resurrection. And our authority problems will be over on the day it is said to us as the devils said to Jesus, "I know who you are — the Holy One of God!"

Fifth Sunday in Ordinary Time: Healing

"Praise the Lord who heals the brokenhearted."

J ob is a case study of one who is in need of healing on all levels. He is suffering from a physical illness and is thus experiencing weakness and pain. But he is also experiencing depression and feelings of worthlessness. He is bitter and tempted to hatred because his friends and lovers have become adversaries and enemies. He experiences all of this as sin in the large sense because he knows that he, righteous as he is, is not exempt. So he cries out. He is helpless. In his isolation he knows that he cannot cure himself. He wants to give up on the world, on himself and on God.

Into this afflicted life, and I take Job to be Everyman and Everywoman, comes the person of Jesus Christ. And Jesus does two things. He preaches good news, and He heals, that is, he makes the good news concrete. He demonstrates it.

To those who are afflicted the very possibility of good news can seem a cruel joke. But when it connects, when once you have experienced it there can be no doubt of its reality. The good news and the healing of Christ are experienced through faith, hope and love.

Through faith we believe in him. Notice that before he works a miracle Jesus always asks faith. He wants us to trust him, to let go of our defenses, to take a risk, to walk on the water. He wants us to begin believing in him and in ourselves.

Through hope he restores our confidence in the future. We begin to see again the possibilities which we in our blindness had ruled out, or which we thought had dried up and were gone for ever. And in this hope we are enabled to work toward a better time.

Through love, his own love which he places in our hearts, we receive a powerful medicine that heals us. Christian charity is simply human love in which God's love is felt. It restores and rebuilds, for it is a love which is not possessive but liberating. It is a gift of grace.

Now this healing which Christ brings is manifest in many ways. We see it in the sacraments, not only in the anointing of the sick but in all the sacraments: in baptism when we are set right with God, in penance when our sins are forgiven, in the eucharist when we are strengthened and nourished. But we also see this healing in relationships which are truly Christian. We heal as Christ healed when we speak as Christ spoke and care as he cared. In the family we do not simply receive the bumps and shocks of living next to one another, we are actors for good or ill in wounding or healing each other.

There is also a place for what is called "faith healing." There is a tradition of miraculous healing in Catholicism. Jesus did it, as we see from today's gospel. Some of the saints were healers. Lourdes is an established part of Catholic life. And there has re-emerged a healing ministry within the charismatic movement. This is not in competition with medical science. If you are sick you should go to the doctor. But there is a spiritual realm which has its impact on the physical. Thus we do not refuse blood transfusions to children, nor do we wait till the very end to pray, after all else has failed.

Let us come to Jesus today. Let us present ourselves to him with all our ailments, all our wounds, and all our sins. Let us call upon him with faith. Let us dare to hope that he will heal us of every weakness. Let us love enough to really trust him. Let us "praise the Lord who heals the brokenhearted."

Sixth Sunday of Ordinary Time: Repentance

"[Lord,] if you will to do so, you can cure me."

The point about leprosy is that we've all got it. We think it a fearful and repulsive thing, and certainly there is that aspect to it. But we're too quick to reassure ourselves that it has nothing to do with us. I don't mean the physical disease of leprosy, which is more properly known as Hansen's Disease. I am thinking of a spiritual leprosy, or what is more properly known as sin.

We are all sinners. There is no surprise in that. We are

all sinners in our own particular way. We have all fallen short of the mark — have all preferred ourselves to Christ and to others. The disease is in our blood. So I take it for granted that the leper in the gospel is me and you. The challenge is to identify with him not in his leprosy but in his faith. "Lord, if you will to do so, you can cure me." His infirmity is nothing remarkable. It is his faith, his daring, his boldness which sets him apart and makes him special.

When we come to know ourselves as sinners we come to know our need to approach Jesus the same way the leper did — on our knees. We come to him and say, "If you will to do so, you can cure me." That is the right way to approach. Not telling the Lord, this is what I am going to do for you, but humbly asking, daring to believe that there is something he can do for us. This is difficult for us because our deep rooted pride gets in the way. We must get around seeing our spiritual life as some kind of project to be organized, managed and carefully negotiated. We must give up the idea that it all depends on us, and that as soon as we can make ourselves good enough God will love us. We are lepers, and against all reason, God already loves us.

The heart of repentance is encountering Jesus Christ. The first step is finding the courage to go to him, fall at his feet and beg his help. But more than beg, we must truly believe that he can help, that he can heal even us. We see him healing lepers, restoring sight to the blind, and making the lame well, yet we do not believe that he can do anything for us. That is because we are either not desperate enough, or not brave enough. We are afraid of what our life would be like if we were truly holy and not so mediocre. We cannot imagine a life of heroic virtue, and we refuse the invitation to it unless it is thrust upon us. Surely there is enough evidence in the gospel to prove to us that we have nothing to fear from Jesus. We must simply take a chance and make a move.

" 'Lord, if you will to do so, you can make me clean.' Moved with pity, Jesus stretched out his hand, touched him, and said, 'I do will it. Be cured.' "

Seventh Sunday of Ordinary Time:
Amen — the name of Jesus

*"It is through him that we address our Amen to God
when we worship together."*

Amen is a little word. We say it all the time and yet it is
an important word. St. Paul says as much by way of a
theological aside in today's epistle. He is defending himself against accusations of fickleness, for he had promised
to visit the Corinthians and then changed his plans. His
enemies now use this against him as an instance of al-
leged inconstancy. His defense is to associate himself with
the fidelity and constancy of God. Paul asserts that his
word has not been " 'yes' one minute and 'no' the next,"
but always "yes," just as Jesus "was never anything but
'yes.' " Paul proclaims that all God's promises under the
first covenant, all God's faithfulness to those promises
have reached fulfillment in Christ, and that is why
"through him . . . we address our Amen to God when we
worship together." This gives us, almost inadvertently, an
important way to understand Christ and an important
way to understand what it is we do when we gather for
worship.

We all learned as children that Amen means "So be it."
If we learned French in school in the old days, we also
learned that French prayers used to end, not with Amen
as they do now, but with *Ainsi soit-il*, "So be it." Amen is a
way for us to punctuate our prayer. Amen means "yes." It
means, "Everything I have just said, or which has been
said in my name, I make it my own, I affirm it." Indeed
we see how in the gospel, when Jesus wishes to underline
his sayings, emphasize and give authority to them, he always begins, "Amen, amen, I say to you."

But Paul deepens and enriches the meaning of Amen.
He says in effect that Jesus is the Amen of God. Jesus is
the one who utters the perfect and final acceptance to the

plan and the promise of God. He does this in all his preaching and healing, and then finally on the cross when he commends his spirit to the Father. Jesus is the Amen of all creation, the new Adam who is obedient even unto death and so triumphs over death and sin. Moreover, Amen is the name of Jesus Christ, or at least one of them. In the Book of Revelation we read, "And to the Angel of the Church of Laodicea write: The words of the Amen, the faithful and true witness, the beginning of God's creation." This refers to Jesus in just this way: Jesus is the Amen of humanity to the salvation God offers.

"It is through [Christ] that we address our Amen to God when we worship together." Jesus is our mediator with the Father. When we say Amen in our prayer and worship we enter into Jesus' Amen. We make it our own, associate ourselves with it. We ratify and extend the assent of Jesus Christ to the grace which God is offering. When we say Amen we are perfecting the creation of God. We reverse the "I will not serve" of Lucifer. We echo the song of the angels and accept in the name of Jesus Christ the "new thing" which God has done in him. Amen is also the very last word of the Bible.

In a way it could be said that the spiritual life entirely consists in repeating over and over these two tiny syllables. Our life is to be an Amen, an Amen which we are constantly making, constantly perfecting, and by which we constantly offer ourselves with Christ to God. "It is through him that we address our Amen to God when we worship together." This Amen is not just the utterance of our throat and lips, it is the sacrifice of our heart and the form of our life. Our daily death and rising, our struggle for faith and for life, our attempts to pray, to give of ourselves, to live for others: this is the Amen of life.

Eighth Sunday of Ordinary Time:
A too spiritual spirituality

*"How can the guests at a wedding fast
as long as the groom is still among them?"*

The idea of heaven that Jesus proposes and the one that most of us have are probably wildly divergent. Jesus keeps describing it in very earthly — not to say earthy — terms: weddings, banquets, parties, among many other similes drawn from life. Yet our culture conventionally sticks to images of angels floating on clouds. This is certainly not a very gospel way to think. So perhaps we may be offended by, or at least try to minimize the imagery we get out of, today's readings. It is very intimate, warm and personal. It has much to do with the body, and at least partly to do with sex, which many of us have been taught to think of as the enemy of spirituality and the antithesis of what is godly.

The first reading has to do with a difficult marriage. Hosea finds in his troubled relationship to Gomer an image of God's troubles with his people. But Hosea is going to try out on his wife God's strategy. The first part of the first appointed verse has been left out of the Lectionary. It goes: "I will allure her" (some translations: seduce her). Then: "I will lead her into the desert and speak to her heart." This is pretty sexy stuff. How does God want us to think of his attitude toward us in our infidelity to him? He whispers into our ear the suggestion of a second honeymoon where he will woo us and romance us and make love to us.

Likewise in the gospel passage we have another earthy image for the presence of Christ among us, the awareness of which is, after all, what we are to cultivate in our prayer life. To the objection of religious people who criticize him for not being stricter and more ascetical with his followers Jesus answers, "How can the guests at a wedding fast as long as the groom is still among them?" Fasting is the last thing you do at a wedding banquet, you eat a lot, drink (maybe) a lot, dance and generally have a good time. Christ is with us; we must rejoice and that must mean living life, and living it well at every level.

But the spirituality we have absorbed, that has seeped into our pores, goes against all of this. Many of us tend to fear becoming too worldly, or if we are already what we judge to be too worldly, we fear we are ineligible for spirituality. We live in a dualist world where the flesh is the enemy of the spirit and the earthly quite hostile to the heavenly. We are taught to be careful, to fear "falling into sin," as we say. We think of spirituality as a different atmosphere, a lighter-than-air gas which a few delicate souls after many years of striving may eventually be able to live on. But that is not it at all.

We have forgotten the reality of the Bible and its quite down-to-earth approach to things. We have forgotten Jesus and his way of communicating, the examples he used, the parables he told. We have forgotten our great Catholic mystical tradition. Forgotten it? We have never known it. Never known how colorful, concrete, sensual is the language of saints about God. Every Christmas we commemorate the feast of the Incarnation, and the meaning of it goes into our ears but never drips down to make connections with the other organs of sense. But God took "flesh" in Jesus Christ. Not my word but St. John's, yet many of us think it is not a very spiritual word since we use it only in one connection.

The point here is that we sometimes try to make our spirituality too spiritual. We forget that God does not save souls but saves us body and soul. We forget that in the phrase of A.M. Allchin "the world is a wedding," and evidently from today's gospel Jesus agrees.

Ninth Sunday of Ordinary Time:
Super Sunday

"That is why the Son of Man is lord even of the sabbath."

The meaning of Sunday is something we may not have considered beyond the simply moral level of whether or not I (or my family) ought to go to church, and are there consequences if I do not? For people individually, as indeed for the Church at large, this is not a trivial question, but it needs to be enriched and re-shaped. Today's scripture shows us a path along which we may deepen our reflection.

First it is necessary to distinguish the Jewish sabbath from the Christian Sunday. They are not the same. The sabbath is presented to us in the reading from Deuteronomy with a twofold rationale: the demands of social justice united with the theological theme of remembering the Exodus. Israel is to keep holy the sabbath day by not working, and therefore not oppressing the work force, since "you too were once slaves in Egypt." The meaning is both practical and theological. The people need to rest from their work. But they also need the leisure to attend to their religious duties, the worship of God. The two motives are linked. The sabbath serves to preserve the memory of their religious history. It reinforces their identity as the people who belong to God, the God who sets slaves free.

The question of the sabbath, its meaning and relative value are raised in the gospel today. Jesus is criticized for permitting his disciples to transgress sabbath regulations about work and travel. He himself dramatically confronts the critics by healing a man and making the radical statement, "The Son of Man is Lord even of the sabbath." These words are evidently so provocative that they are not recorded by Matthew or Luke. Scholars indicate that this passage reflects the early Church's conflict with the

Jewish community over sabbath observance. The Church, especially after it began to think of itself as something other than a movement within Judaism, changed its worship day from Saturday to Sunday, from sabbath to Sunday.

It is important to see that unlike the Jewish sabbath, the Christian Sunday was not and is not essentially a day of rest. It became so only after Constantine made Sunday the weekly rest day. This is not to say that a rest day is not important individually and socially. It is merely to notice that for several centuries the early Christians, who were mostly of the slave and laboring classes in the Roman Empire, routinely went off to work on Sunday.

Sunday commemorates the Resurrection. It is centered on Christ. Clearly it owes a lot to the weekly sabbath, but it is a different day precisely to distinguish a different community and to highlight that community's unique creed: Jesus Christ, the Son of God, was crucified for our sins and raised for our justification. "That is why the Son of Man is Lord even of the sabbath." Moreover, the Christian Sunday has an eschatological character, that is, it points to the kingdom of God which is beyond time. As the sabbath is the seventh day, falling at the end of the "week" of creation, so Sunday is the eighth day, the day beyond the week, the day of the *new* creation. The eucharist is celebrated on Sunday as a sign of the heavenly banquet which we await, but of which we now enjoy a foretaste.

But there is also that in our Sunday which is quite congruent with the Jewish sabbath, especially as presented in today's first reading. It keeps alive for us and in us our identity as the called-out people of God. We gather to remember, to tell the story, to read out from the scriptures the history of God's dealings with men and women. We gather to break the bread of Word and Sacrament so that we may have strength to continue our journey.

Lastly, the ancient Christian writers called Sunday the day of joy. Following them let us re-echo the words of today's psalm refrain: "Sing with joy to God our help."

Tenth Sunday of Ordinary Time:
Shame, blame and salvation

*"I heard you in the garden; but I was afraid,
because I was naked, so I hid myself."*

What a crooked tribe we humans can be. Take Adam
and Eve. Their story, the story of the Fall, is meant to account for our deep-seated perversity, our infallible ability
to get things wrong, to leave our smudgy fingerprints on
everything lovely. The story of the Fall is not pretty, but
is full of pathos. It is we at our worst, a story of shame and
blame. Shame makes Adam hide from God. Shame makes
him shift the blame onto Eve, and Eve to blame the serpent.

Why so? Our hunger for transcendence sometimes
goes awry. Creation is good but we let it master us; we
misuse it. We get greedy and never stop wanting. We take
what does not belong to us and what is not good for us.
We try to fill up our inner void with all kinds of "stuff"
(things, and people used as things) we think will make us
happy. It never does, but we never stop. And when we are
confronted with the truth, as Adam and Eve were, we
deny it just like them. We cast the blame elsewhere, or we
hide from God and from the truth. We drink from
poisoned wells and insist it is sweet water. We kill ourselves by inches and protest we are having a great time.
We turn on one another and justify it as the way life is.
Who will free us from our destructive behavior? Who will
save us from our sin?

Well, Jesus, of course. But how do we treat him?
"When his family heard of this they came to take charge
of him, saying, 'He is out of his mind'; while the scribes
who arrived from Jerusalem asserted, 'He is possessed by
Beelzebul,' and 'He expels demons with the help of the
prince of demons.' " Here is a verse we don't remember
and which has not entered our piety. Here is an embarrassed attempt by Jesus' family (not further identified) to

manage him, to finesse an awkward moment. Isn't it just another tint of Adam and Eve's shame they feel? Jesus is too brutally honest for them. He delves into things polite people leave alone. He's on again about sin and evil. He's too simplistic; doesn't understand the compromises folks have to make. Go along to get along. No, not him; stands out like a sore thumb. Draws attention to himself. Still worse, he actually tries to do something. He's powerful and therefore dangerous. He takes on Satan toe to toe. Mighty confident, isn't he?

Here we are: Adam and Eve, Jesus' family, afraid of our shadow, hiding behind the trees, still sewing fig leaves, hating the serpent but still doing deals with him. And here is Jesus: stronger than demons, unafraid of truth, speaking in parables, setting people free. What have we to lose? He invites us: "These are my mother and my brothers. Whoever does the will of God is brother and sister and mother to me."

Eleventh Sunday of the Year: Vital signs

*"By means of many such parables he taught them
the message in a way they could understand."*

There seems to be scant evidence in this world of the kingdom of God, the reign of God over human hearts. Just pick up a newspaper or look at TV. It always seems to be a week of murder, tragedy and corruption, of accidents and crimes. Left to our own devices we might soon turn sour, and give in to pessimistic and cynical despair. There is just not much to show for two thousand years of Christianity. Or is there?

It was to confront an experience like ours that the writers of the New Testament preserved such memories of Jesus as we hear in today's gospel. These are two parables of the kingdom, two signs for discovering what it is that Jesus means when he talks about the reign of God. These parables are meant to answer the question of the second generation of disciples: "Why has not the message of Christ taken the world by storm? Why is there still evil in the world? Why does the Church always promise more than it can deliver?"

The temptation is to think that the spiritual power of the gospel is illusory and really trivial; that the message of Christ is idealistic but naive; that Christ himself is dead and has no power over this world. The answer is that the kingdom of Christ is truly at work in the world, but in a hidden way; that Christ reigns, but from a tree; that the Lord has assumed the guise of a servant. The message of today's gospel is that the kingdom is at work in the world, but cannot be measured by it. We cannot quantify the success of God. God will not be squeezed into our one-pint cups; will not stand still for our measuring tapes; is too fast for our stop watches; will not be numbered by our computers.

For just as seed planted in the earth seems to all outward show to be deader than dead, and yet has the potential for life within its dried-up hulls, so the seed of the Beatitudes, the kernels of Christ's teaching about the kingdom, a teaching rejected by the world, is nonetheless transforming it. Once more we are reminded that we cannot go by appearances. We must not see the way the world sees, nor judge the way the world judges. There are positive and hopeful signs all around. In my ministry as a priest I am given the grace to see them every day. They seldom grab headlines, nor are they captured on videotape for the late news. The French writer St. Exupery has his Little Prince say, "What is essential is invisible to the eye." And in the same vein, Georges Bernanos in *The Diary of a Country Priest* says, "Grace is everywhere." One must acquire the eyes of faith, the insight, the inner sight to see it.

Recently I had a day in which my eyes were opened and I saw much, a day in which I celebrated five of the seven sacraments, all signs of the kingdom and disclosures of the hidden life thriving beneath the surface.

At 8:15 a.m. I celebrated the funeral Mass of an 85-year-old woman. Her body lay in the middle aisle where just the week before had lain the body of a bishop. And like him, she was surrounded by a faithful family praying for her soul, mourning for her, and commending her to God. What a touching sight.

At ten I witnessed the marriage vows and prayed the nuptial blessing over a man and woman in their sixties. What a sign of hope and grace that was. What a sign that God does not want us to be alone, but has made us for one another.

After lunch that day I baptized a little boy whose adoption had recently been finalized. A wonderful sign of new life for him, and a sign to me of a husband and wife whose hearts were big enough to make room for another in their home.

At 2:45 p.m. I was called to the bedside of a dying woman. Her family joined in the prayers as she was anointed and the Commendation of the Dying recited. It was a sad moment but also a moving one, a moment full of faith and full of grace.

At 4:00 p.m. confessions began and penitents made their way to the boxes, convinced of their sins but more convinced of God's loving forgiveness.

Is there little evidence of God's kingdom in the world? You'll never convince me of that. I've seen too much, and so have you. The signs of it are all about if only we have the eyes to see. "By means of many such parables he taught them the message in a way they could understand." May the Lord open our eyes.

Twelfth Sunday of Ordinary Time:
Love casts out fear

"Why are you so terrified? Why are you lacking in faith?"

Franklin Delano Roosevelt had this to say in his first inaugural address, March 4, 1933: "Let me assert my firm belief that the only thing we have to fear is fear itself — nameless, unreasoning terror which paralyzes needed efforts to convert retreat into advance." The account of the storm on the lake is the human story of love faltering on account of fear.

Storms are known to be sudden and fierce on Lake Gennesareth. There is no reason to believe that the account is exaggerated. Have you been to sea in rough weather? The most I can say is that I've crewed for my brother on the little sloop he used to sail on the Great South Bay of Long Island. On a puffy day with the hull heeled over and the water coming over the rail you can get nervous, especially if you're inexperienced. And if the wind shifts and you jibe, and a following sea comes over the transom, you'd better be able to depend on your seamanship.

But these men of Jesus' crew were experienced hands. They were professional fishermen. They had seen rough weather before, and had reason enough to be afraid. Jesus' rebuke to them must seem sharp: "Why are you so terrified? Why are you lacking in faith?" Then at a word from Jesus the wind fell off and the sea grew calm. Christ's power was shown forth; his sovereignty made manifest. And where does this take place? That night it was seen in the jaws of an angry sea. It was seen midst the fury of the storm. It was seen where the need was greatest and the absence most bitterly felt.

The disciples were in danger that night. But the most serious threat was not the weather, nor was it the leaky boat. Rather, it was the temptation to give up; the temptation to yield to fear. It was that "nameless, unreasoning terror which paralyzes" about which Roosevelt (who understood paralysis) warned. Fear incapacitates. Unless something else overrides it, it short-circuits the system. The temptation is always to yield to fear — or depression, or cynicism or callousness. But "love bears all things, believes all things, hopes all things, endures all things." And Love rebuked the wind, and the storm died down.

You and I are full of fears and neuroses and compulsions and God knows what else. Their name is legion for they are many. But we are also full of dreams and wishes. Full of hopes and possibilities. Full of grace. Full of the Spirit who casts out fear. Full of faith and love which the Lord has planted in our hearts. These are the things we must believe in. Believe in Jesus. After all, "Who is this that even the wind and the sea obey him?" He is in the boat with us. He will calm our fears and make us strong.

Thirteenth Sunday of Ordinary Time: Trust overcoming fear

"Why bother the Teacher further?"

Self-hatred is a destructive emotion even when it is not carried to its absolute and irrevocable limit, suicide. Self-hatred takes many forms. It destroys healthy human relationships or cripples their beginnings. It makes people sick in mind and body. And because it is a human problem it is also a spiritual problem. It belongs to the realm of what needs healing and what needs salvation. For example, it can keep from praying, that is, from trusting God. Listen to the people from the synagogue official's house. They arrive with the news that his daughter is dead and they add the sorrowful comment, "Why bother the Teacher further?" This question can be read on several levels. It can simply be frustration and loss of hope. Death is final; it is obvious that no more can be done. But the question also reveals the people's need to distance themselves from Jairus' appeal to Jesus. They are embarrassed by it. It is the desperate act of a dignified servant of the synagogue. It is not the "done thing" to go running after scruffy itinerant rabbis, even when they have reputations as healers. But Jairus is desperate. He loves his little daughter. To him it is worth it.

But there is another way to hear the remark "Why bother the Teacher further?" Sometimes aren't we afraid to "bother" Jesus because we think too little of ourselves? We feel we are unworthy of his time and attention. It is hard for us to believe he could be interested in us. We are too sinful, too stupid, too unattractive, too ordinary. After all, Jesus is a celebrity and I am a nobody. He doesn't know I'm alive. Or, we dare to hope for some attention but are afraid of the exposure it will mean for us. I don't want God scrutinizing me too closely because he will discover how seedy I really am and then he'll really hate me. And the unspoken part added under our breath is, "as I hate myself."

Isn't it true that we refrain from praying because we feel unworthy of it? We would feel like hypocrites to pray. God would laugh at our prayer. You've got to be good to pray. When I'm better (morally, spiritually, physically), then I'll pray. This is what we feel, and this is what we think. But the gospel gives us another idea. The woman with the hemorrhage, after twelve years of misery, felt she had nothing left to lose. She wanted to encounter Jesus the healer and she wanted to do it quietly. When it couldn't be managed quietly, St. Mark says she became "fearful and began to tremble," but she broke through to salvation. She was healed in body and spirit. "Daughter, it is your faith that has cured you. Go in peace and be free of this illness." And Jairus too was fearful because Jesus says to him, "Fear is useless. What is needed is trust." And Jesus thought it not a bother, and so Jairus' daughter was raised.

We must not be too polite with God. We must take a

chance and be daring like these characters in the gospel. We must think enough of ourselves not to make excuses like "Why bother the teacher further?" We must overcome fear and learn to trust. We must dare to believe that God loves us, even us. We must learn to love ourselves as God loves us. We must learn to "bother the Teacher."

Fourteenth Sunday of Ordinary Time: Measuring success

". . . when I am powerless, it is then that I am strong."

Today we hear of three men who would never make the cover of *Business Week* or *Time*; three men who experienced human failure, rejection and weakness. And yet we read about and listen to them, we hold them up for imitation because by our lights they were great successes. We call them saints, and one we call the Son of God.

The prophet Ezekiel faced opposition and was rejected by his people. When God called him to be a prophet he did not promise him fulfillment, fame or popularity, and Ezekiel received none of these. Instead he was rejected, for what he had to say was unwelcome and unpleasant. But Ezekiel resolved to prophesy anyway, "whether they heed or resist." In human terms he was a failure, rejected by his audience.

St. Paul is better known to us. In today's passage he speaks rather personally about his troubles. He describes them as "a thorn in the flesh, an angel of Satan to beat me and keep me from getting proud." Nobody knows exactly what he means. There have been many guesses which range from physical maladies, to mental depression, to more lurid suppositions. Various commentaries offer a full range of opinions. In the absence of certainty I have come to agree with the German exegete Lietzmann, who remarked, "The trouble is the patient has been dead for nineteen hundred years and diagnosis is now difficult!"

No matter what it was, what is singularly remarkable is Paul's attitude toward this affliction, this "thorn in the flesh." "I am content," he says, "with weakness, with mistreatment, with distress, with persecutions and difficulties for the sake of Christ; for when I am powerless it is then that I am strong." An exceptional attitude that, and one which does not come naturally to us humans.

Then there is Jesus. Today's gospel portrays him returning to his own part of the country. Does he receive the jubilant welcome home of the local hero? Not at all. "Where did he get all this?" they say. He is greeted with sarcasm and rejection. He is written off as a carpenter who has gotten above himself. The gospel says, "They found him too much for them." A literal translation would be "They were scandalized in him." And a *skandalon* (Greek) is a stumbling block, an obstacle placed in one's path, something to tangle your feet and bring you down. St. Mark closes with a terse and utterly tragic comment: "He could work no miracle there, . . . so much did their lack of faith distress him."

The story of these three failures makes me ask myself what I think about success and failure. Have I not absorbed certain attitudes toward success from the world around me? Have I not made assumptions which are suggested by the material prosperity of this time and place, and which are daily reinforced by advertising and the values promoted by the media? Don't I own an idea of success which is not entirely in tune with the gospel, and which makes me see Ezekiel, Paul and Jesus precisely as unsuccessful, as failures?

We think of America as the land of unbounded opportunity, as that splendid experiment in popular democracy and freedom, unparalleled in human history. For this we want to be thankful, but we tend to forget that the bulk of humanity does not share in the same blessing or abundance. We tend to forget that most of our ancestors came here in steerage, and some in chains. We tend to think of success in a limited way. Most often we are thinking of success in post-war, suburban American terms. We think of the standard of living which we know. Our temptation is to identify America with the Promised Land of the Bible, or as the kingdom of God, which it most surely is not. We must learn to be thankful, but not idolatrous. We must learn and remember our history.

Ezekiel and Paul and Jesus help us to examine our lives in a different light. They help us to recognize our actual priorities, and to re-measure our idea of success; to see beyond material prosperity, and suburbia, or Yuppie values, whatever they are supposed to be. Ezekiel and Paul and Jesus help us to remember how fragile the human enterprise is. When we must contend with being let go, with the uncertainties of financial markets, the incredible pressures of "the job," with the real cost in terms of family relationships, the hazard of alcohol or drug abuse, the temptation to compromise ethical standards: when this is what happens to the American dream, Ezekiel and Paul and Jesus offer an outside audit.

These three make us ask the hard questions. How do we deal with the darker side of life? How do we define failure? Am I a failure if I don't have all the nice things TV and magazines say I should have? If I don't have the right car, or the right label in my clothes or membership in the right club, do these lacks make me a failure? Am I really a failure if I have not increased the profit margin of my division by X per cent; or if I don't make AVP by September; or if I am not invited to this party or invited to work on that project?

The gospel stands human values on their head. St. Paul says, "When I am powerless it is then that I am strong." Paul also says, "We preach Christ crucified." In our profession of faith we all stand up and say that the first, last and only perfectly fulfilled human being "was crucified under Pontius Pilate, he suffered, died and was buried." And then we are expected to go out and live as if we really mean it. We both know that is not easy. Perhaps that is why we return here each week: to be confronted — and comforted — by the gospel. To place what passes for success in our lives on the paten, and to pour out what we fear and know is failure into the chalice. We offer them to God so that they may be changed, so that they may be lifted up to him, so that they and we may be consecrated and become an oblation approved and acceptable, an offering in spirit and in truth.

Like Ezekiel, may Spirit enter into us so that we may know the real difference between success and failure. Like Paul, may we willingly boast of our weakness that the power of Christ may rest upon us. Like Jesus, may we lay our hands on the sick of heart and lift them up to God.

===

Fifteenth Sunday of Ordinary Time: The trip of a lifetime

"Justice shall walk before him,
and salvation, along the way of his steps."

Travel has come a long way from the days when only the rich could afford it, when servants packed trunk after trunk and lugged it hither and yon, when the only way to Europe was by ship, and the "grand tour" was a once-in-a-lifetime experience for the privileged few. Technology has changed all of that. Jumbo jets have replaced ocean liners. Plastic bank cards have replaced letters of credit and gold sovereigns. Super apex economy has replaced POSH class. Nylon garment bags have replaced wooden trunks. Travel has become faster, easier and accessible to all.

In today's gospel Jesus sends the disciples on a journey. He wants them to travel light, lighter even than we do today. Jesus gives none of the practical advice of Fodor, Fielding or Baedeker. His edition of "The Holy Land Guide" is far more severe. They are not simply restricted to carry-on baggage; they are to take "no traveling bag" at all. Not only no American Express card ("Don't leave home without it"), but he says "not a coin in the purses in their belts." No reservations for the second sitting at the captain's table, no expectation of McDonald's at the next freeway exit ("E-Z OFF and E-Z ON"). They are, however, permitted sandals and walking stick. Even Jesus appreciates how important a comfortable and sturdy pair of shoes are to the traveler.

The point here is more than whimsical. Jesus is sending the Twelve on mission. It is not a vacation, but a business trip. They are told to leave the baggage at home for a reason. It is not penitential, but it is ascetical. Travel always has an element of risk. After all, we leave the familiar surroundings of home and venture off into the unknown. Most of us respond to that by taking "home" along with us. We over-pack, especially if we are inexperienced travelers. In attempting to eliminate the risk, we take too much. We take our Walkman and our Watchman, our cassette deck and CD player, our fourteen favorite magazines, a year's worth of novels, twenty changes of clothing, even our own "bathroom tissue." And why? "Because you never know what you will find when you go abroad. Best not to take any chances."

Jesus doesn't permit the Twelve such luxuries or illusions. They must go unencumbered. Reason is, it must be seen that what they say (the heralding of God's reign) and what they do (the healing of the sick) is done not by human ingenuity, not by dint of effort, not by superior logistical support, but by God working in them. What they do is done by grace. Clearly the journey is an image of life itself. And this missionary journey, set as it is in the midst of the public ministry of Christ, is a trial run for the mission of the Church. It must be established from the start that the work of preaching the gospel is no mere human endeavor, but God's initiative and God's design.

To accept the call to discipleship, therefore, requires the emptying of self. To be a follower of Jesus means enterprising a risky journey. Not only must we anticipate the mishaps and snafus which inevitably accompany travel, we must count on them. Jesus' journey led him to Jerusalem and the cross. Our destination, though it is the heavenly Jerusalem, has a stopover in the earthly city, and Calvary is on our itinerary. There are no direct flights in the kingdom, no cut-rate fares, no cheap day-returns. If you book with Jesus and his company, you must commit to the whole package, your luggage restrictions will be very severe, you will not be staying at first-class hotels — but you will have the experience of a lifetime.

So let us journey with Jesus. May we be happy to be known as companions of his. May he speed our journey toward his kingdom. May today's psalm find fulfillment in us: "Justice shall walk before [them], and salvation along the way of [their] steps."

Sixteenth Sunday of Ordinary Time: Priests like Jesus

"I will appoint shepherds for them who will shepherd them so that they need no longer fear and tremble . . ."

Today we might reflect with profit on Jesus our priest, and on the ministry of priests among us. Today's scripture readings teach us much about this.

Jeremiah shows us in prophecy that it was God's plan to send his Son to look for us and find us and gather us into his kingdom. The image he uses to describe this work of salvation is that of a shepherd. He says in the first reading, "I myself will gather the remnant of the flock . . . I will appoint shepherds for them. . . ." God is speaking through Jeremiah about the prophets, and also in prophecy about his Son, about Jesus, when he says, "I will raise up a righteous shoot to David . . . he will do what is just and save the land."

So in the first place, when we think about what a priest is, we must think about Jesus, who Jesus is and what Jesus does. He is sent from the eternal Father to gather us together and bring us to God. Jesus is our shepherd and our priest, our great high priest, who leads us to God. Curiously, in the entire New Testament the apostles and their helpers are never called priests. The first Christians understood Jesus to be *the* priest, and so that term was reserved for him.

And just how does Jesus fulfill his role as priest? St. Paul sets it out for us in the second reading. He says, "In Christ Jesus you who once were far off have been brought near through the blood of Christ." That is, by his cross and passion, by his resurrection and ascension, he reconciles us with God. He makes us who were once estranged from God, cut off from God, enemies of God, to be close to God, friends of God, daughters and sons of God. In a word, "It is he who is our peace . . . [he who] came and announced the good news of peace . . . [so that] through him we both have access in one Spirit to the Father." This is the mission and ministry of Christ.

Now the work of earthly priests, like the priests in your parish and diocese, is meant to imitate the work of Christ, to echo it and carry it forward. The work of a priest is the same as Christ's work: to lead people to God. Traditionally this is described as a threefold ministry: prophet, priest and king. Or in other words: teacher, pray-er, pastor. These three facets of the priest's work are illustrated in the beautiful psalm which we pray today:

The Lord is my shepherd; there is nothing I shall want.

A priest must be a teacher and evangelist. He must show people their true shepherd who is Jesus. He must proclaim the love of God over and over again, like Jesus who took pity on the crowd and "began to teach them at great length." People want to know about God. They need to hear that God loves them, forgives their sins, gives them eternal life.

He guides me along right paths, for his name's sake . . .
With your rod and your staff that give me courage.

The priest is to be a leader. His voice must have the authority which only deep faith in Christ and faithfulness to his teaching can give. It is not easy to lead people. All of us prefer to choose our own path and go our own way. The priest's job is to keep us together on the "right path."

You spread a table before me . . .
You anoint my head with oil.

These lines remind us of the sacraments: the eucharist, Christ's banquet which the priest prepares and presides over in Christ's name; and the anointing of baptism, confirmation and the sacrament of the sick. Think too of the ministry of reconciliation which we experience in confession. Is this not an anointing with the tender mercy of Christ?

Pray for your priests. Pray that they may be faithful to the work of Christ which is their calling. Pray that the condemnation of Jeremiah against "the shepherds who mislead and scatter the flock of my pasture," may never fall upon them. But pray that they may be good shepherds. May they heed the invitation of Jesus to go aside in prayer each day to that "out-of-the-way place and rest a little." May they have the heart of Christ who was moved with love for the people "because they were like sheep without a shepherd."

Seventeenth Sunday of Ordinary Time: The food connection

"The hand of the Lord feeds us; he answers all our needs."

If we take time to notice some things about food and our experience of eating, we will appreciate the more this marvelous story of Jesus' miraculous feeding of the crowd.

1. *About food and hunger.* A meal tastes better if you

have an appetite for it. Cooking is more appreciated by those who are hungry. "Hi, mom! What's on the stove? When are we going to eat? I'm starved." The basic purpose of food is to provide nourishment, to sustain us, to keep us alive and well. Yet many of us are eating ourselves into an early grave, literally killing ourselves with food. We have become more alert to the dangers of cholesterol, the need for fiber in the diet, the relationship between poor nutrition and heart disease and cancer. We are discovering that it is better on many scores to be a little lean, a little hungry.

The disciples manifest a similar attitude. They "kept following [Jesus] because they saw the signs he was performing for the sick." They had a hunger of the spirit, a hunger for meaning and wholeness, and they recognized who could fill them. Yet even they misinterpret; they want to make Jesus king. How important to know where the true hunger lies. That is why we fast before communion. "The hand of the *Lord* feeds us; *he* answers all our needs."

2. *About food and fellowship.* One of my professors at Notre Dame used to say that as far as food consumption goes, there are three levels: feeding, eating and dining. Feeding is what happens when you sprinkle the flakes into your aquarium and the fish come up to gobble. Feeding is what happens when kids eat without tasting in order to get back to their games or the TV.

Eating is what you will likely do after Mass. The ordinary family meal falls into the range of eating. It may be informal and unfancy, but some amenities are observed. The meal is taken seated at a table. It is eaten from plates, and knives and forks are employed. Conversation accompanies it. People excuse themselves if they have to leave for some reason.

Dining, on the other hand, is something really special. It is more than just eating out; true dining is reserved for special occasions (like Thanksgiving, Christmas, and wedding anniversaries). It is formal, may be accompanied by candlelight, special costume, and normally requires the better part of an evening. It is a ritual in every sense. And while considerable attention may be paid to the menu, it is really the fellowship, the conversation, the sharing, the meaningful occasion which claims attention.

American fast food (along with television) has been the most powerful solvent of the ancient bond between food and fellowship in the family. All the same, it is heartening to see that when teenagers go to the local burger joint it is not so much because of the french fries as to hang out and be together. What the coffee house was to Dr. Johnson and Samuel Pepys, the pizza parlor or the yogurt cafe has become to the young people of today. Food provides the setting for gathering people together.

So also for the disciples of Jesus. This miracle story of the feeding of the multitude, which has echoes of the eucharist, is not just about the practical problem of providing for hungry people. It is about feeding them and uniting them in still deeper ways. What is important in our experience of the eucharist is not merely the food but especially the fellowship, that is, the communion. And it is not only what happens between me and Jesus, but necessarily also what happens between me and you.

That is why St. Paul, in the earliest recorded expression of outrage at a sacrilegious communion, lambastes the Corinthians for having their fill while others in the same hall go hungry. They sin against Christ because they sin against the needy among them. They fail to discern the body of Christ in their brothers and sisters, and so fail to discern it in the sacrament. They have made the eucharist as private, as coolly detached, as anonymous as picking up that sack of burgers at the drive-through window. "I got mine. I don't really care about you." "The hand of the Lord feeds *us*; he answers all *our* needs."

3. *Food and love.* Everyone has the image of the Jewish mother who plies her children with ever greater helpings of corned beef and matzoh ball soup. But she doesn't have to be Jewish. The Italian mother says, "Mangia!" The Belgian mother says, "Smakelijk eten!" The American mother: "Have some more. Don't be shy. Eat up." Cooking is an act of love. Perhaps it is not always practiced wisely, but the connection is there and we have each experienced it.

So also the disciples. The holy table is a groaning board filled to overflowing with the tokens of God's love. The feast of the kingdom is fulsome, for the love of God is boundless. Indeed, there are leftovers. ". . . they gathered twelve baskets full of pieces left over by those who had been fed by the five barley loaves." Leftovers are a problem, but not to the imaginative cook — or the imaginative Christian. So many are hungry, and we have so much. So many are loveless, and we have been loved so much. So many are needy, and we have plenty to share. "The hand of the Lord feeds us; he answers all our needs."

Eighteenth Sunday of Ordinary Time: True devotion

"This is the work of God: have faith in the One he sent."

What is it that we seek from God and from our faith? What is it that we are looking for and expect? What have we set our hearts on? What do we pray for? What? Or who? The gospel reading prompts these questions. The crowd sought out Jesus. They were very interested in him. They chased after him across a lake, made inquiries and were most persistent in tracking him down. Yet Jesus is skeptical of their motivation, and questions their real reasons for seeking him.

First he says that they are only interested in him because they have had their fill of the bread that he multiplied. They recognize a good thing when they see it, but they seek him only for what they can get out of him. Jesus throws them off the trail by insisting that they work not for earthly food, perishable food, but "for food that remains unto eternal life."

He is leading them along. At first they are like children who love Christmas simply because it means presents, and lots of them. They are entirely absorbed in the gifts themselves. Later on the children will grow up and come to value what the gift means. Their focus will shift from the gift to the giver. So Jesus is drawing their attention toward himself.

Well, they are willing enough to work for the "food that remains unto eternal life" without understanding exactly what this means. They ask, "What must we do to perform the works of God?" And Jesus says, "This is the work of God: have faith in the one he sent . . . [and] . . . I myself am the bread of life." What he asks of them he likewise demands of us.

If we are to be mature Christians, if we are to grow up in our understanding and practice of the faith, our attention must begin to shift from signs and wonders and peripheral matters to the heart of the matter, to an intimate relationship of faith and love in the one on whom "the Father has set his seal." This means that our attention must be shifted from the gift to the giver, from ourselves to our savior, and likewise from ourselves toward our brothers and sisters.

There are many people in the world who live a superficially religious life, but avoid the harrowing encounter with the living God. They live out their religious convictions either in a superstitious way or at a level of devotion that remains mechanical and impersonal. If superstitious, they may, for example, take astrology or "new age" philosophy seriously, and believe that their little rituals with horoscopes or crystals can alter that which they see as what an impersonal fate or karma has dealt them.

If they get along in life through an imperfect and limited form of Christian or even Catholic devotion, they may, for example, leave chain prayers around the church. "Say this prayer nine times a day for nine days and St. X won't let you down." But such conditional prayers as these are not the mark of true intercession. St. X winds up being treated like the token clerk at the toll booth, and God is regarded as completely impersonal and ready to be manipulated by the mechanical saying of a complex roster of prayers. All of the trappings of this kind of imperfect devotion fail to bring one close to God. Indeed they seem to have exactly the opposite effect. God is rendered safe and impotent, removed from the danger zone of real contact with me.

Yes, devotion is important. Yes, the prayer of intercession is valid and necessary. But lively intercession and true devotion proceed from another premise altogether. They begin with simple faith, loving obedience and heartfelt trust in Jesus, Son of God and savior. "This is the work of God: have faith in the one he sent." It is when I know Jesus in a personal way as my savior, as the One on whom the Father has set his seal, as the forgiveness of my sins, as my bread of life, it is then that my moral striving, my struggle to keep the commandments and do what is right finds its ground. It is then that I begin to see other people no longer as an obstacle to piety but the manifestation of Jesus' face. It is then that my devotion leads me to God instead of neutralizing God and keeping God at arm's length.

Jesus asks for faith. And when we believe, then shall we know. And when we know, then shall we love. And when we love, then shall we say with the psalmist:

> What we have heard and know
> and what our fathers have declared to us,
> We will declare to the generation to come
> the glorious deeds of the Lord and his strength
> and the wonders he has wrought.

Nineteenth Sunday of Ordinary Time: Food for the journey

"The bread I will give is my flesh, for the life of the world."

Traveling is not what it used to be. It is far easier, far safer and far more convenient. No need now to organize caravans months in advance; one simply picks up the telephone and reserves a flight and a hotel room. Likewise, eating along the route has become quite safe and predictable. The traveler's fare, once an uncertain thing at best, is now (thanks to American processing technology and marketing savvy) almost completely standardized and predictable. This includes the menus in turnpike restaurants, the microwaved miracles brought to your airplane seat, and the Big Mac that is handed over just as quickly in Ghent, Belgium as Long Island, U.S.A. The only difference is that in Ghent you may have your Big Mac with a beer.

They have taken the uncertainty and risk out of traveler's fare, and also the unexpected delights. Food for the journey used to be one of the great travel adventures. Food is familiar and to the traveler represents both home and the strange new places he or she is visiting. Will there be some place to eat in the odd and uncharted parts where I am going? Will what is offered be appetizing or revolting? Will the water be potable and without after-effects? (One observes that Montezuma has taken new revenge in a TV commercial wherein an Hispanic family professes to love America except for the indigestion that comes from eating our hot dogs. All is fair in love and advertising.) Fundamentally, the question of foreign food is not only the uncertainty of unfamiliar surroundings, but also the threat to life and health, and to the journey itself. We must all eat to keep going, to keep up our strength, to continue our journey. "An army marches on its stomach," said the great Prussian strategist Karl von Clausewitz. He was right.

The Bible is full of stories about food and danger, food and journeys: Adam and Eve with the apple in the garden (their last meal before being forced out onto the road); Moses and the Israelites with the manna in the desert (a life-saver for them, though they grumbled nonetheless); Elijah and the hearthcake on his way to Horeb (in today's first reading); and Jesus and his discourse on the Bread of Life.

To come right to the point: the gospel confirms for us something we already know, that we need food for the journey, that the traveler's fare is most important. And the food offered for our journey through life, our trek toward eternal life, is Jesus himself. "I myself am the living bread come down from heaven. If anyone eats this bread he shall live forever; the bread I will give is my flesh for the life of the world."

Therefore we may think of our Sunday assembly as the roadside meeting of travelers. We are pilgrims who break their journey and refresh themselves for the next stage. We are taking our several roads but we are *en route* toward the same destination. We journey in the same direction. We meet to look at the map and swap stories. We take a meal together so that we may have the strength to continue. For though we be pilgrims and sojourners, our wayside meal is assured: Jesus, the living bread for the life of the world. Jesus in the eucharist, the *esca viatorum*, the food of wayfarers.

Twentieth Sunday of Ordinary Time: Paschal food

". . . he who feeds on my flesh and drinks my blood has life eternal, and I will raise him up on the last day."

On the face of it, it was a simple thing that Jesus did on the night before he died. He took bread and wine, said the blessing over it, and gave it to his disciples to eat. He did what the head of any Jewish household did and still does in the course of the Seder meal of Passover. But he did a bit more than that. He identified himself with those elements. He described the bread and wine as his flesh and blood. That was something unprecedented in the experience of his hearers, something bold and startlingly new.

Jesus goes even one step further. He commands the

disciples to eat this bread and drink this wine in remembrance of him. But he says it in a more daring, a more outrageous way. He says, "He who feeds on my flesh and drinks my blood has life eternal, and I will raise him up on the last day." Forget for a moment the devotional way in which you have heard and understood those words for so many years. Imagine that you know nothing of the eucharist and must take those words at face value, must take them literally. How would you feel if someone told you that you must eat their flesh and drink their blood?

The reality of that language and its revolting grossness prove an obstacle to the disciples, as we shall see in next week's gospel. At the same time that language, strong as it is, uncompromising as it is, is an assurance to us about Jesus' seriousness in giving himself in the sacrament that we now know as the eucharist. The realism of it is unmistakable, and what is more, it is sacrificial language. In making the bread and wine his own flesh and blood, and in bidding us to eat and drink it, he is linking four realities in an unbreakable bond: himself, his death on Calvary, the bread and wine, and us.

We participate in him by eating his bread and wine. But because he has made the bread and wine his flesh and blood, our participation is far deeper, more intimate. To eat his flesh and drink his blood is to participate in his sacrifice. For it is Christ's death on the cross that gives life to the world. And it is the power of his cross which we share when we eat his flesh and drink his blood. So you see, the message of the cross is inescapable. And receiving holy communion is not a safe and pious religious exercise. It is to confront life and death in the most elemental way. It is to experience everything that is in a fragment of bread and a sip of wine. It is to stand at the foot of Calvary and feel its power. It is to taste and see the goodness of the Lord.

Jesus says, "This is the bread that came down from heaven . . . the [one] who feeds on this bread shall live forever." May God make us worthy to eat at his holy table.

Twenty-First Sunday of Ordinary Time: Mutual deference

"Defer to one another out of reverence for Christ. Wives should be submissive to their husbands . . . Husbands, love your wives . . . This is a great foreshadowing; I mean that it refers to Christ and the church."

"Wives should be submissive to their husbands." In these latter days the words of the apostle have acquired a controversial, even a polemical tone. They make a lot of people angry. For feminists they have become a provocation. There are lectors who refuse to read them. Nonetheless these are important words, words worth our attention. We need to think about this epistle, and reflect on the difficulty it poses by appearing to demean women.

First, we must examine the text, recognizing that it is precisely a translation. There is a saying, "translator — traitor," and it is true in this case, for reference must be made to the original Greek. Verse 22: "Wives should be submissive to their husbands." The Greek does not say this. In Greek, there is no verb in this sentence. The verb which is implied is beyond doubt the verb in the preceding verse, "Defer to one another out of reverence to Christ." This verb may justly be translated "be submissive," or "be subject to," as the Revised Standard Version translates. But in context, "Defer to one another out of reverence to Christ" is clearly a general principle applicable to all, men as well as women. It is announced as a subject heading, summarizing the verses which follow.

This casts the difficulty in a new light. Paul is really saying that self-effacement, self-sacrifice, lack of self-interest should characterize all our relationships *in Christ*. For example, wives to their husbands, husbands to their wives, children to their parents, slaves to their masters, and so on. Paul is working out the implications of a comparison between the relationship of wives and husbands on the one hand, and the relationship of Christ and the Church on the other.

But in so doing he incorporates, or at least reflects, the social attitudes and practices of his day and of the centuries right up to our own. That is the problem. Underlying the theological principle, to which we shall return, is a concrete fact of life in his first-century Mediterranean world, and of our world right up till now. Paul reports and reflects the view that women were and ought to remain inferior to men in important ways. Today these social roles are in the process of rapid change in our Western culture. Many people applaud that; some resist it. Many today say that this structure is oppressive and still in vigor; others even hope that it will ever remain so. However that may be, it is not the main point of Paul's teaching. He is not speaking sociologically but theologically. He takes the existential reality for what it evidently is. He makes no attempt to abolish or even criticize it, but he does offer advice on how these important personal and social relationships must be transformed from the inside out. This is the valuable part of the teaching, and what we must concentrate on.

Paul is illustrating a point about mutuality. What he says about both husband and wife are illustrations of a larger, overarching principle, a principle he sets out in his first sentence: "Defer to one another out of reverence for Christ." As we saw, both "defer" and "be submissive" are different renderings of a single Greek verb. "Be submissive" is an accurate but unhappy translation because of its connotations. Paul would not approve the way Stanley treats Stella in *A Street Car Named Desire*, nor of any other abusive domestic scene.

"Submissive wives" and "loving husbands" are meant as concrete instances of deferring to one another. In other words, spouses should be mutually giving and forgiving; mutually caring and forbearing. They should look out for one another, not for "number one." They must sacrifice for one another. They must try to be selfless rather than selfish, whether that is in the kitchen, in the bedroom, or in the living room of their life together. "Submitting" and "loving" modify and complement each other and should be attributes of husbands and wives equally. They are different descriptions of the same reality.

The real power of this passage comes from its basis in our relationship to Jesus. That is what is distinctly Christian about it, and what makes it worthy of our esteem and emulation.

Wives (and surely husbands too) should be submissive because the Church is submissive to Christ. Start with that experience, the experience of discipleship, the surrender of ourselves to God which we make in prayer and worship every day. You kneel down, bow your head, address Jesus as your "Lord," humbly confess to him your sins and your littleness. Then you give over to him your life, your heart, your self in an act of submission which is in no way degrading, but intimate, tender, "heart-deep" and total. Is that not also the way it is to be between spouses? Is that not like the loving surrender of self which is meant in marriage?

Husbands (and clearly wives too) should be loving because Christ loves the Church. Once again what is meant? Start with Christ and see if the experience is not reflected, does not find an echo in the human experience of a happy marriage. The love which Jesus exampled is this: he gave his life for us; he died on the cross for us. That is love's meaning, or as the Anglican writer W.H. Vanstone puts it, that is "love's endeavor, love's expense."

And is that so very different from the love of parents for their children? Or the self-sacrifice of children for aged and invalided parents? Or the fidelity and devotion of spouses to one another?

I was privileged to take communion to a beautiful couple who had reached their nineties together. They were for me the best commentary on what Ephesians 5:21-32 is about, far more persuasive than all the Greek vocabulary or syntax. She was not well for a very long time — chronically ill, in and out of hospital. And truth to tell, he was not so spry himself. But the way that they loved each other, deferred to each other, cared for and encouraged each other, prayed *for* and *with* each other was a true sacrament, or as Paul says "a great foreshadowing."

101

When I went to that house I knew myself to be surrounded by the presence of Christ just as surely as when I kneel before the tabernacle.

"Defer to one another out of reverence for Christ. Wives should be submissive to their husbands . . . Husbands love your wives . . . This is a great foreshadowing; I mean that it refers to Christ and the Church."

Twenty-Second Sunday of Ordinary Time: Filling the abyss

"God is greater than our hearts."

In today's gospel Jesus says that "wicked designs come from the deep recesses of the heart." It sounds rather reminiscent of the old radio show which began, "Who knows what evil lurks in the hearts of men? The shadow knows [sinister laugh]!" And I thought of the cartoon of the old miser opening his wallet and moths flying out. That's the human heart, full of dark secrets and terrible truths which only God and psychoanalysts can read.

Is the human heart evil? I don't really think so. And I don't think Jesus is saying so either. But he is stating a profound psychological and spiritual truth. Here is how the late Dominican writer Gerald Vann put it: "The heart of man is an abyss. There is room in it for infinity because in it there is an infinity of desire; and it cannot remain empty; the stark horror of alien evil will inhabit it if it is not filled by the limitless ocean of the goodness of God."

The Catholic tradition is fairly optimistic about human nature. But it is also realistic. It believes in people's basic goodness but it is ready to admit that men and women inflict much pain and suffering and are quite capable of great wickedness. There is such a thing as human hatred which is deliberate, calculated and murderous. But most of the time when we get off the track, when we fail morally, it is because we are going about the right task in the wrong way. Misguidedly we try to fill up that abyss with things, or with people used as things.

Let us take, for example, some of the vices listed by St. Mark. Greed. Our possessions are a way for us to assert our status, to say "I'm somebody" when inside we feel like nobody. We struggle to achieve, to get, to have. We work hard; we buy; we store up; we are consumers. And once we get, we scramble to keep, to defend, to protect. We worry and go without sleep because our passions have come to possess us.

It matters not whether what we have is large or small. When I was in the seminary I was meditating one day on poverty of spirit, and I thought I was pretty detached. I was dependent on the bishop's indulgence in paying my tuition and board after ordination, dependent on scholarships for summer music school, dependent on my family for pocket money to keep me in candy bars. All I had to my name was a couple of cassocks and a few books. I was the proverbial penniless student. But what about those books? I had to admit I was pretty attached to them. They were not worth much in themselves. Barnes and Noble would have given only a few dollars for them. But I was proud of them and used to display them so that other students coming into my room would have to say, "Here lives a scholar equal to Erasmus or St. Jerome." I had more books than I could read, but God help you if you borrowed one without asking me. The heart is an abyss which not even the Library of Congress or the British Museum can fill.

St. Mark also mentions sensuality. The integration of one's sexuality is one of the great projects of adult life, and it offers plenty of room for mistakes. With sexual as with other sins, it is not that people are depraved, for the most part, but rather that they let their desires and their hunger to be esteemed and appreciated get the best of them. The Russian Orthodox bishop Anthony Bloom, in his wonderful book *Beginning to Pray*, says that "the sins of the flesh are the sins the spirit commits against the flesh." He says that our imagination is like tentacles spreading over people and things which makes us imprisoned to things, glued to them. He says:

> You will be like Gulliver, knit to the ground by one hair and another hair and another hair. Each of the hairs is really nothing, but the sum total will keep you solidly tied down. Once you have allowed your imagination full sway, things are much more difficult. In that respect we must be sober and fight for freedom. There is a great deal of difference between attachment and love, between hunger and greed, between live interest and curiosity, and so forth.

What do we do with these hungry hearts of ours? There is one who is able to fill the abyss, for he (as St. John says) is greater than our hearts. And of all the things in this world which are attractive and desirable but impossible of attaining, he is not. The one thing we can pray for and know that we shall receive is he himself — the living God.

God asks for your heart and mine today. Let us put our hearts into the chalice with Jesus' heart. Let us lift up our hearts to the Lord, offering them to him. For "the heart of man is an abyss; there is room in it for infinity because in it is an infinity of desire. . . ." And God wants to fill us with the limitless ocean of his goodness.

Twenty-Third Sunday of Ordinary Time: Equal before God

"Did not God choose those who are poor in the eyes of the world to be rich in faith and heirs of the kingdom he promised to those who love him?"

"All men are created equal," so says the American Constitution. It was a radical notion in the 18th century and it remains radical today. On one level there are many nations which do not profess universal equality even in theory. South Africa is a ready example, a nation much in the news and much in our prayers. In South Africa discrimination is not just a *de facto* condition, it is state policy, for the Black majority is denied equal rights and is hemmed in on every side by a comprehensive web of repressive laws. And, despite much that is hopeful in the recent past, it is much the same in many countries of the world. America, to its credit, is based on the ideal of equality. Like most ideals the reality continually falls short of the theory, but it is at least a fundamental touchstone of the American dream. Success is not guaranteed but "life, liberty and the pursuit of happiness" is part of the Constitution.

In the realm of everyday living, however, it should be perfectly obvious that all men and women are *not* created equal, and are not treated as equals even in America. There is a very great difference from person to person in talent, industry and intelligence. There is a great difference in what each starts out with, what handicaps each must overcome, and what each does for him- or herself. On a practical, empirical scale it is perhaps more true to say that all are created unequal in wealth, talent and opportunity. All are meant to be equal in the law. But we know that the rich have greater access to first-class legal representation. All have an equal right to basic education. But we know that ghetto schools cannot hold a candle to suburban ones. All have a right to work. But the unskilled or semi-skilled worker is more likely to be unemployed and for longer than the engineer, the computer programmer, or the college-educated professional. Life is unequal.

St. James, the author of today's epistle, knows this. He is writing to a parish that included both rich and poor members. Probably most of the first Christians were what today would be called "socially disadvantaged," to use a polite term that masks the reality of what being poor really means. For the most part the early Christians were not blue-collar workers, they were slaves. But a few were rich; a few belonged to the merchant class; and a few had gotten ahead. It is these whom James addresses in today's reading. "You must not think of yourselves as any better than those others," he tells them. There is to be no favoritism. He is not denying that differences exist; rather he is going underneath differences. James is cutting the legs off the illusion of superiority which money and education and social standing bestow. He is saying that there is something more basic, something which under-cuts all that makes us appear unequal.

We are radically equal because we all stand in need of the grace of God. All of us are sinners, the poor and the rich alike. All are loved by God, for Christ died for all. What is different is merely external; it is a veneer. It seems important in the world, but the world is wrong. In the view of eternity we each have the same destiny; we each will face the same judge; we each will be held to account. In view of eternity we are quite equal, radically equal.

St. James reminds this congregation of their roots. "Did not God choose those who are poor in the eyes of the world to be rich in faith and heirs of the kingdom he promised to those who love him?" The basis for Christian social justice is not a political theory but our radical equality before God. We must love the poor because Jesus loves them. We must view them the way Jesus does, as the least of his brothers and sisters. We must act toward them the way he does, which is the same way he acts toward us: mercifully and charitably, justly and generously.

If you have seen the film *Romero*, which chronicles the life of El Salvador's martyred archbishop, you know there are many chilling scenes in it, scenes of brutality, torture and murder. One of the most disheartening occurs com-pletely without blood or manifest violence. A young aris-tocratic woman, a woman whose family has been close to Monseñor Romero and whose husband has been mur-dered by the guerrillas despite the archbishop's interven-tion, comes to him to arrange for the baptism of her baby. The archbishop quickly agrees and invites her to come to the cathedral on her chosen Sunday to have the baby bap-tized along with all the other children. Puzzled, she asks for a private baptism. He refuses. "You mean," she says with shock and disgust, "my baby will have to be baptized with those Indians!?" "Yes," he answers — and she stalks off in anger.

We face many temptations in our journey through life. One is the temptation to think ourselves better than others. It is a very human failing; perhaps we are more prone to it the more successful we become. This is the temptation to be too self-reliant, to believe too much in our own efforts and accomplishments, and to look down on everyone else. Our temptation is the temptation to forget, to forget who we really are, to forget all the help we had along the way, to forget that we are the poor person, to forget that God made us rich in faith.

May God fill us with a love for his poor. May he give us tender hearts and lively consciences toward them. May he open our eyes to see how radically equal we all are in his sight.

===

Twenty-Fourth Sunday of Ordinary Time: The sacrifice of the heart

"Whoever would save his life will lose it, but whoever loses his life for my sake and the gospel's will save it."

Peter's confession of faith, the appointed gospel for today, so full of dramatic tension, is a turning point in the ministry of Jesus. Peter's confession poses for us the dramatic questions which we must face in our own lives. First, our Lord asks who people say he is. Peter is forthright. There is little risk in answering such a question, even were the answer to be unpleasant. Peter is merely reporting, and it is not necessary for him to endorse the varying responses.

But Jesus is not satisfied and soon raises the stakes. "And *you*," he went on to ask, "who do you say that I am?"

Now it is getting more interesting. Peter will have to declare himself, for the next answer counts. Peter's palms begin to sweat but he is exhilarated all the same. "You are the Messiah!" he proclaims. And we say, "Well done, Peter, you've got it right." We feel proud of him and just a little self-satisfied, like parents watching their child succeeding in school or at sports. Peter's answer reflects well on us. We know the answer and believe ourselves ready to give it when it is our turn to be asked.

Yet again Jesus ups the ante. Peter squirms. His face flushes and his pulse quickens. Jesus "began to teach them that the Son of Man had to suffer much, be rejected, . . . be put to death, and rise three days later." This is too much for Peter, so he pulls Jesus aside and tries to talk some sense into him. We might imagine their conversation going like this. Peter: "Look Jesus, you don't have to get fanatical about this. You're doing just fine. Sure, the scribes and the Pharisees are a problem, but our people can get to them. That problem can be handled. If we play our cards right there will be no suffering, well, nearly none. You're the biggest thing to hit this country since . . ." But his voice trails off because Jesus is just staring at him resolutely. Jesus just isn't buying it, and is in fact getting very angry, until finally: "Get out of my sight, you satan! You are not judging by God's standards but by human standards!"

Later Peter might complain privately, "If only Jesus weren't so demanding, so absolute. If only he didn't press his luck. If only he knew a little about public relations. If he just had a press agent, a media manager, all of the nastiness of Calvary could have been avoided." That is Peter's view and often we share it with him. Quite naturally we always want to take the easy way, the path of least resistance. Go along to get along. We don't want to make a fuss; don't want to upset the apple cart; and certainly don't want to die. That is the difference between Jesus and Peter, and the difference between Jesus and us.

There is already so much suffering in life, who would want more? No healthy person, that's sure. The cross is repulsive and we will turn away from it every time. Death is frightful and we will avert our glance from it repeatedly. Taking up the cross is something we do only when there is no other option, or only for a while (like Lent), and then only in a trivial and token way. That is the way we are. Peter is us right down to the toenails. Jesus knows that about us, but he still won't let us off the hook. Gentle and tender as he is, he would be untrue to us if he did not offer to share with us everything, including his cross and passion. Perhaps it is only after we have known suffering that we begin to see his wisdom in it. I do not mean in a Stoic, stiff-upper-lip sort of way, "We all have to suffer so it might as well be for some noble cause." It is much deeper than that. It is the mystery of life and death. How finely those two are intertwined. The young and the inexperienced at living may not yet have discovered that. Death does not exist for them. And yet age is no guarantee of complaisance in that great mystery. I fear that dead though I be, I'll still kick and scream when they try to put the lid on my casket. The poet says, "Do not go gentle into that good night," and most of us are in full agreement.

In the end it has to do with love and trust. The questions which Jesus puts to Peter are asked in a certain order, and that progression is crucial. The final question, the one about suffering and death, can be faced only if the preceding one has been got right. I cannot face the cross if I have no faith in Christ. I cannot take up my cross if I have no confidence in him who was nailed to his. I cannot deny my very self and lose my life if I do not trust him who promises to hold my life in his hands. The cross is no abstraction, and you and I will not climb onto it for some noble cause or lofty philosophy. But we may do so out of love. We will for some*one*. We will because we believe that he who lost his life has saved it. We will if we can muster the trust that goes along with the bold confession, "You are the Christ, the Son of the living God."

We will and we have. It is lived everyday in thousands of undramatic, but nonetheless heroic ways. It is lived in the fidelity of marriages, and in the fidelity of priestly ministries. It is lived in the heartfelt care of sick parents, spouses or children. It is lived in the hunger for justice and solidarity with the poor. The confession and the cross are lived in the struggle to speak the truth in love, the struggle to speak to God in prayer, the struggle to go on working in a job you hate and in the struggle to make the best of a situation in which there are no options. The confession is made and the cross taken up when we own up to our sin; when we acknowledge that we have been shirkers and have said, "I know not the man." It comes to pass when in tears we confess our fear and our weakness; when on our knees we give up the pretense of playing at being God, and let God be God. It finds fulfillment in us when suddenly, we know not how, we do the unexpected, the selfless thing; when we feel grace course through us like lightning; when we are surprised at our conductivity of God's purpose.

When the priest pours the wine into the chalice, pour out your heart there. And when at the end of the Eucharistic prayer he lifts the paten and the cup in a gesture of offering to the Father, offer your heart and mind, your body and soul to God. Be lifted up even as Jesus was lifted up on the cross. So may God make us an acceptable sacrifice and an offering approved.

Twenty-Fifth Sunday of Ordinary Time: Stay tuned

"Though they failed to understand his words, they were afraid to question him."

The point of today's gospel is to direct the disciples, both those of long ago and ourselves, to the cross and to lives of service. This is now the second time in St. Mark's gospel that Jesus has predicted his passion. He says, "The Son of Man is going to be delivered into the hands of men who will put him to death." And the disciples, if they are to be faithful to their master, will have to put to death their self-interest. For he likewise says, "If anyone wishes to rank first, he must remain the last one of all, and the servant of all."

But there is more. There is a bit of "business" between Jesus and the disciples which we can pick up if we listen closely. It has to do with the ability to communicate and the willingness to listen. After the prediction of the passion we read this: "[The disciples] though they failed to understand his words . . . were afraid to question him." That reaction is all too familiar. They were afraid. And you recognize the kind of fear which afflicted them. It was like the fear of a woman who has detected a lump in her breast and puts off going to the doctor for fear of the news that it might be cancer. It is an irrational but all too understandable fear. If the growth is malignant it can't be getting any better while she waits, but if it is benign she is subjecting herself to useless anxiety. Yet we all know someone who has done just this.

It is the same fear which inhibits students from asking their teacher a question in class. They don't want to appear stupid. Maybe the explanation they need had been given a few moments before while they were distracted. So they shut up, hoping that the light will go on. But the teacher, in her own ignorance of their ignorance, plows right on and very little teaching or learning happens.

Then we see that it is not only fear which cripples these disciples; there is something else. When they arrive home Jesus asks what they were discussing along the way. But "at this they fell silent, for on the way they had been arguing about who was the most important." You know that silence. It is the silence of the child caught red-handed filching a couple of dollars from his mother's purse. It is the blushing silence of embarrassment when our actions not only speak louder, but even make words impossible. The disciples had been tuned to a different channel altogether. It had become impossible for them to hear what Jesus was saying about his suffering and death. They were unable to be present to him, unable to share this most important thing which he had to say to them because they were unable or unwilling to listen.

He might have responded as we would, indignantly, self-righteously and with a storm of anger. He might have withdrawn into the protective ooze of self-pity. He might have allowed the estrangement which had grown between him and them to harden into alienation and bitterness. He might have, but he didn't. Instead he reaches out to them in a very gentle and accepting way. He takes a child into his embrace and demonstrates his response in a wonderfully human and telling way. And because of who he is, that response is not simply human but divine. It is the human expression of God's acceptance of us, the human model for our response to God and each other.

Fear and guilt, self-righteousness and hurt are barriers to communication, to effective sharing, to a more abundant life. They short-circuit the communion of life which God means us to enjoy with one another and which is the foretaste of that communion which he means us to have with him. Let us ask him to break down those barriers which we set up in our hearts, the defense works which insulate us from life's joys and pains and from God's grace. Let us make our own the prayer of John Donne in his *Holy Sonnet V*:

Batter my heart, three-personed God; for You
As yet but knock, breathe, shine, and seek to mend;
That I may rise and stand, o'erthrow me, and bend
Your force to break, blow, burn and make me new.

Take me to You, imprison me, for I
Except you enthrall me, never shall be free,
Nor ever chaste, except you ravish me.

Twenty-Sixth Sunday of Ordinary Time: The inclusive circle

"By their fruits you will know them."

Life is full of boundaries and generally they serve a useful purpose. A mother says to her child, "Don't go off the block." Or to a teenager, "Be home by eleven." The boundary is given for the sake of protection and so that the child will learn self-discipline. In the same way a manager says to a salesman, "Your territory is Metro New York." Or a bishop says to a priest, "I am assigning you to the parish of St. Ignotus." The boundary is meant to help define and achieve the purposes of the organization, be that sales or pastoral care. Boundaries help us develop identity and direction. They help us know who we are and where we are going.

Sometimes boundaries lose their reference and become ends in themselves. This is illustrated in today's first reading and gospel. Moses imparts the spirit on the seventy elders and they prophesy. But along come Eldad and Medad who were not in the tent of meeting and had not received Moses' authorization. Yet they prophesy too. A *young* man objects, "They are not approved; stop them." The detail is persuasive. The young are frequently full of enthusiasm and idealism, and have not yet learned that life is rarely tidy, and often quite messy indeed. Things seldom work out exactly the way they are supposed. Moses intervenes. He tells them not to be jealous, for it is the effect or the net result that counts. "Would that all the people of the Lord were prophets."

Likewise today's gospel tells the story of a strange exorcist. He expels demons by the power of Jesus' name but he is not a regular disciple. "We tried to stop him because he is not of our company." The disciples sound like lawyers for a famous soft-drink company going after a trademark infringer. You can't call your hamburger stand "McDonald's" if you haven't got a franchise license. But

Jesus, just as Moses before him, has a broader view. Says he, "Anyone who is not against us is with us." In other words, look at the net result.

There is a lesson in this for us. We are Catholics and we ought to be proud of it. We are the heirs of a great spiritual tradition. But if we are truly secure in our faith then we need not be threatened by other religious groups. We ought not feel jealous of their successes, or be suspicious of their motivations and programs. Sometimes people criticize the Church, saying, "We're becoming too Protestant." I doubt that people who say that really understand Protestants and perhaps don't even know any. They seem defensive as if it were a shameful thing to admit that a Catholic ever learned anything from a Protestant. I'm proud to say that I've learned lots from Protestants and I hope it has made me a better Catholic, a better Christian.

The same may be said of our attitudes to adherents of other faiths. "Those Jews think they're so great. God's chosen people!" people say. Or "You know the Jews would never let anybody get away with that." There may even be a grudging admiration in such a remark, making it into a left-handed compliment. But deep down there is resentment, and fear, and prejudice. Such people choose to live with the illusions of stereotypes and caricatures. They prefer cartoon versions to reality. Catholics above all should be sensitive to this since we have so often been the victims of it both in the past and the present.

I am not saying that one religion is as good as another and it doesn't matter what you believe. If I thought that, I would choose a less demanding faith than Roman Catholicism. What I am saying is that we can take a lesson from Moses and Jesus and welcome truth and goodness wherever we find it. We can look at the net result. We can use Jesus' yardstick: "By their fruits you will know them."

The poet Edwin Markham put it this way:

He drew a circle that shut me out —
Heretic, rebel, a thing to flout.
But Love and I had the wit to win:
We drew a circle that took him in.

114

Twenty-Seventh Sunday of Ordinary Time:
Forever

"Let no man separate what God has joined."

It is a truism to say that ours is a world of rapid social and technological change. Newspaper and magazine ads offer us ever newer and more amazing machines: TVs, microwave ovens, computers. *Scientific American* and even *Popular Mechanics* display a future of technological advance still in the dream stage. The pace of change has become ever faster and the need to adapt produces ever more stress.

"Let no man separate what God has joined." These words of Jesus about the permanence of marriage are demanding in an age where nothing is permanent and everything changes. In the midst of a world where only the new seems to be interesting, Jesus tells us to stay with the old. When our catchwords are "update," "modernize," "go with the flow," he tells us to stick with the original. When the message of business, education and the media is "be flexible," "keep your options open," and "get rid of obsolescent equipment," Jesus says, "Let no man separate what God has joined."

The prohibition of divorce stops us right in our tracks. It is so demanding, so contrary to what we see and know, so much against the grain. Many of our contemporaries would say it's way out of date. But Jesus is quite definite and the Church holds to it. It is a hard teaching and a lofty challenge. What value can it have? What does it mean?

Everyone knows that marriage is a reflection of God's love and a sharing in it. The permanence of the marriage bond, what the Church calls its sacramental character, is precisely this, that it is a sign of God's love, a love that is everlasting. God is faithful to us. God won't stop loving us, ever. No matter what we may do; no matter how unfaithful, how wayward we may be, God keeps on loving us. And this love is given to us in all the sacraments, not least in the sacrament of marriage. That is why it is to be forever. The "forever" of the marriage vows is an echo of God's "forever" to us. It is meant as an earnest of the "forever" that awaits us in heaven, until we take possession of it.

Neither is it automatic, as well we know. It requires much effort and real commitment. It demands faith. Both spouses must believe in themselves, in each other, and in their future together. They must believe in marriage in general and in their own marriage above all. They must learn to recognize the presence of Christ in one another and be ready to believe that he will be there for them "for richer or for poorer, in sickness and in health."

Jesus invites husbands and wives to make an absolute commitment to each other; he challenges them to the kind of total giving he showed when he laid down his life. That is not something the world understands, for the world is always provisional, passing and pragmatic. Marriage in Christ is for life. The values of the world are for the time being. Christian marriage is for now and for time to come. It is a sign of the kingdom in the world, and we pray that it may be "on earth as it is in heaven."

That is why marriage is a sacrament and a vocation. It is a way of being a disciple, a way of following Christ in the world. And that is why the family is called the "domestic Church," because it is the family of God in miniature. It is where reconciliation heals estrangement, where togetherness drives out loneliness, where life is nurtured and children are "formed by the gospel" and "have a place in [God's] family."

This is the vision of marriage which the gospel proposes to us. It is important that we hear it, rehearse it, and recommit ourselves to it. When we get caught up in the humdrum and the struggles of everyday it is sometimes possible for the vision to cloud over, and we forget the things that once were so vivid for us. In this way the gospel renews our hope.

But we must also be mindful of those for whom the vision has already perished, those whose marriages have failed. We must be concerned for them not out of any

116

superiority or smugness, but simply because our Lord
loves them none the less. There is as much healing
needed in their lives as in anyone else's. And perhaps
they have now found another but the Church is unable to
recognize that union.

Let us hear the Lord's call to fidelity and permanence.
Let us also re-dedicate ourselves to the sacredness of all
life, most especially to that which is more and more
threatened — the unborn and the elderly. Let us make
the words of the psalmist our own: "May the Lord bless
[husbands and wives] all the days of [their] lives."

Twenty-Eighth Sunday of Ordinary Time: Rich in compassion

*"There is one thing more you must do. Go and
sell what you have and give to the poor . . .
After that come and follow me."*

The reading of this gospel always leaves me unsettled.
Jesus' encounter with the rich young man somehow goes
awry. We've all had that experience, meetings that start
full of promise but are booby-trapped by conflicting ex-
pectations and missed signals, conversations with many
words but little communication. We have had encounters
where what we have wanted most of all is to make a good
impression on a special someone and we go away convinced that what we made was a complete ass of ourselves.

It could be that the rich young man was looking to be
praised. Perhaps he was trying to insinuate himself into
Jesus' circle, so he promotes himself. Do you not detect a
little coldness and suspicion in Jesus' remark, "why do
you call me good?" It sounds like he is trying to keep the
guy at arm's length.

On the other hand, we may take this young man as perfectly sincere. The gospel usually alerts us to phoneys with a set-up line like "In order to trap Jesus they asked him such and such," but there is no hint of that here. I rather think he was an earnest young man, very serious and full of enthusiasm, but he is also quite innocent of experience. He is a man who has the world in his pocket and is soon to discover just how much he has yet to learn — about life and most especially about himself.

Yes, he has kept the commandments. There can be no doubt of his goodness. He is moral and upright, a regular straight arrow. What a fine son-in-law he'd make, and you'd hire him into your firm tomorrow. But Jesus pulls the rug out from under him. "There is one more thing you must do. Go and sell what you have and give to the poor . . . after that come and follow me." In a flash all his optimism is gone. The tables have been turned. His breath is taken away. There are no words, no excuses, nothing. His "face fell. He went away sad, for he had many possessions."

The heart of the matter, I think, is not that he was rich in a material way; that is almost incidental. For there are rich people who are very detached and poor people who are very covetous. His downfall, I believe, is that he wants salvation on his own terms. He will be a disciple his way, rather than Jesus'. He will be holy as he sees fit, not as God sees. He is a self-made man in every way, but in the kingdom there are no self-made men.

Perhaps he thinks of the poor and the sinner in comparison to himself. "If I can do it, why can't they?" Perhaps some of us think of the poor and the sinner in like terms. Also we may want to deal with God like this rich young man. We are good so we expect God to play by the rules and leave us alone. We think of God like we think of the IRS: if I am straightforward and don't take too many questionable deductions maybe I won't get audited, maybe God won't look too close.

We prefer the illusion that we are in control of our lives. It is important for us to maintain at least the appearance that everything is cool, everything is OK, everything is under control. We adopt the liberal ideal that given enough time, money, good will and hard work we can save ourselves and the whole world. But it just isn't so.

Keeping the commandments is essential. We must know them and do them. But Jesus asks more: "Go sell what you have and give to the poor." It can mean many things. Above all it means learning to trust God, really trust him. Most of us do not trust him, we fear him. We learn trust only as a last resort, only when our life or the life of a loved one is at stake. Trusting God is a form of poverty because it means that we believe God loves us not because we are good, not because we give a lot to worthy causes, not because we're Catholic, but just because he made us and makes us lovable.

"Go sell what you have" may mean learning compassion for the welfare mother, the illegal alien, the mentally handicapped. Compassion is different from condescension. With compassion I discover that I am fundamentally like the other in some essential way. I may not be mentally handicapped but I am handicapped emotionally, or socially. I may not be on welfare but I understand what it is to be dependent in a humiliating way. I may not be an alien but I remember what it feels like to be snubbed, to be excluded, to be told I'm not wanted.

Then again, "Go sell what you have" may *literally* mean "Go sell what you have." It is not impossible that God may be calling some one or other of us to a life of radical poverty. Someone of the younger generation may be called to be a missionary in a Third World country. Someone of the older generation may have to give up their house one day soon to go live in a single room in a nursing home. Someone here may lose their job, their investments and have to begin life over on a lower economic level. Such scenes can be seen either as tragedies or as opportunities, and God only knows how we would respond to such a turn of events. What we *can* do is to live inwardly and outwardly a little more detached from our goods and from our goodness. We can also learn compassion for the rich young man of the gospel and see that he may be me.

119

Twenty-Ninth Sunday of Ordinary Time: Celebrities or servants?

"Anyone among you who aspires to greatness must serve the rest; whoever wants to rank first among you must serve the needs of all."

Have you considered the cost of celebrity? Our newspapers and TV screens are full of celebrities; we can't get enough of them. We eat them for breakfast, lunch and dinner. We watch *Entertainment Tonight* because for us entertainment is not only what celebrities do on stage; we crave the drama of the celebrity personality itself, a life larger than our own, and more exciting — or so we hope. It is the same with politicians, who, with the collusion of the media, have turned themselves into celebrities. They are briefed and groomed, "managed" like prize fighters, "handled" like theatrical talent, taught how to dress, to walk, talk and smile. They rise and fall by the "sound bite," the quotable phrase, the "camera op," which is fodder for the voracious electronic pet-monster we keep chained to our living room electric outlets.

But what is the cost to them, to the politician and the TV star? We have seen the assassination of civil leaders, the murder and maiming of screen stars by deranged fans. What about the stripping bare of family life, the brutal denial of privacy? The stress of the press conference with shark-like reporters in their feeding frenzy to fill the bellies of presses and videotape machines? What becomes of the human wounded left by the roadside as the campaign moves on to other fronts? What is the human cost of that?

Harry Truman said that you ought to stay out of the kitchen if you can't stand the heat, and politicians necessarily have to have tough hides. I'm sure the politicians we see are plenty tough, but there must also be a real humanity under the facade. Sometimes, as you sit and watch the political process, you ask yourself who would want to go through the hell of it to be President, mayor or anything?

Of course no one knows how tough life is going to get. If we did we'd likely all be paralyzed into inaction. Sometimes, when it gets really hectic in the parish and people are climbing up my back about one thing or another, I begin to regret that I did not follow my first instinct to become a Benedictine monk. There is a certain cost to being a public persona, and the inflation of modern life is driving that cost up everyday. At times I feel a great empathy with Garrison Keillor and his radio friends in the fictitious Lake Wobegon, Minnesota. He advertises "powder milk biscuits which give shy persons the strength to get up and do what needs to be done."

In today's gospel we see two seekers after celebrity, James and John. They are ambitious and not at all shy. They recognize that position is everything, and they want to be in the picture when Jesus makes the front page of the *Jerusalem Post*. They want to be important. More than that they want to be *seen* to be important. Like many who aspire they don't know what they're in for, but they soon find out what Jesus thinks about power and prestige. "Anyone among you who aspires to greatness must serve the rest; whoever wants to rank first among you must serve the needs of all."

Power and authority are necessary. The world won't work without them, and neither will the Church. I suppose I'll go on wondering why anyone in their right mind would seek public office, but I am profoundly grateful that someone is willing to put up with it. But for us Christians, whether we are in public life or private, whether we are outgoing or shy, power and authority must be exercised as a form of service. For "the Son of Man came not to be served but to serve — to give his life as a ransom for the many."

There are many applications we could make of this as regards our common life in a Christian community, and doubtless change would have to follow in the way pastoral efforts are organized, how meetings are run, how priorities are set. The point of the teaching, then, is not whether there should be authority but how it should be exercised. To that end we have quite a bit of guidance, not only this gospel, but the whole of canon law — 1752 canons — and many diocesan and parish policies and guidelines. But law may set only a minimum standard. The gospel calls us to do more.

The gospel calls us to live by the Spirit. And it calls us to live this way both in our personal and our institutional life. I may indeed be a shy person who avoids public responsibility, but at the same time I may be (or could become) a little Hitler with my own family and among my intimate circle. It is possible for us to use the authority of our state in life selfishly, in order to satisfy our ego. We can "lord it over people," or think ourselves superior, or use them to make us look like big shots. This can be so whether we are a spouse, parent, supervisor, or manager. It always remains a temptation.

James and John asked to be seated first, highest and nearest. In time they will realize that they are asking the wrong question. Jesus offers them to drink of his cup, and he means the cup of suffering. Can they drink it? Can they drink it down to its bitter dregs? He offers that cup also to us. "This is the cup of my blood, the blood of the new and eternal covenant. It will be shed for you and for all so that sins may be forgiven." Our communion is a participation in the passion of Christ. This is the true cost of service for the sake of the kingdom.

In the end it is not a matter of whether we are bold or shy, whether we are ambitious for office or cling to the shadows of anonymity. If we do not live a life of service in the way Jesus proposes we will find ourself left out at the last. If in our serving we turn away from the cross, it will come to find us; and the cup that is passed will eventually come around to us. What matters then is the quality of our serving and how we carry our cross. Let us serve Christ and serve alongside him. Let us, above all, serve him in his least brothers and sisters.

Thirtieth Sunday of Ordinary Time: Blind, yet seeing aright

"Son of David, have pity on me!"

The story of the blind man along the road is touching because it holds so many hopes and possibilities for us. We may not recognize this at first, but it is remarkable how very like Bartimaeus we are or must become. We may at first be put off by him, a pathetic figure, a blind beggar. Perhaps we have seen him in the bus or train station, and he is not at all appealing. He is filthy and strange, horrid looking and foul smelling. But look a little closer. Bartimaeus is us in our sinfulness and brokenness before God.

Unlike Bartimaeus, relatively few of us are physically handicapped. Few are blind or crippled. Few of us are poor in absolute terms. Begging is a degradation to us and we would be ashamed to be reduced to it. Still, Bartimaeus is our brother. He asks for sight. "Rabboni, I want to see." This demand can be ours too. Are we lacking sight? Perhaps we are, only our prayer is: Lord, that I may see myself as you see me. Lord, that I may see the suffering and the need of those around me. Lord, that I may see what I should pray for and what I should do. Lord, that I may see you coming to me.

Also, Bartimaeus seems so uncouth both to us and to the bystanders who scold him. But he is undaunted. He embarrasses us with his unvarnished directness and his unmannerly calling out. "Son of David, have pity on me!" For a blind man he sees pretty well where his help is from. His cry and the words of his prayer go right to the heart, a blind man who hits the target every time. Would that our prayer were so honest, so true, so unceasing.

In fact the words of his prayer have acquired the weight of a great spiritual tradition. "Lord Jesus Christ, Son of God, have mercy on me, a sinner." This version of Bartimaeus' cry has come to be known as the "Jesus prayer." It plays a very important part in the spirituality of Eastern Orthodox Christians, and is one of the acts of contrition proposed to us in the new rite of Penance. There is a tradition that it is by means of this prayer that Christians can fulfill the command of Jesus to pray without ceasing. The habit of reciting the prayer slowly, over and over again, can lead to its becoming a very deep part of our spirituality, so that praying it can become as natural as breathing.

Bartimaeus received his sight, and when we leave him in this scene he is following Jesus up the road. That must be our way too. Jesus encounters us on the road of life. If we are brave enough to confess our sins and ask his mercy he will surely heal us. And then he says to us, "Come follow me." But be warned. He is headed toward Jerusalem. He is headed to the cross and to Calvary. That is where the road of discipleship leads. If only, like Bartimaeus, we could see that we have nothing to lose and everything to gain. If only we could see that what we leave behind is only our blindness and brokenness.

For the road of discipleship is hard, but it is also full of joy. We have the option of staying by the roadside with our begging bowl. Or we may receive our sight, get up and journey on to the new world Jesus promises to those who love him. Let us choose to follow Jesus. With the psalmist let us say, "The Lord has done great things for us; we are filled with joy." Let us say with Bartimaeus, "Lord Jesus Christ, Son of God, have mercy on me, a sinner."

Thirty-First Sunday of Ordinary Time: Our Jewish heritage

"Shema Yisroel, Adonoy elohenu, Adonoy ehod."
"Hear, O Israel! The Lord is our God; the Lord alone!"

These words from the book of Deuteronomy, which Jesus repeats in the gospel today, constitute the Hebrew creed. They are recited in prayer by Jews every day, morning and evening. In so doing they are affirming their faith and linking themselves with their ancestors over the generations and the centuries. When we say them they are linking us to Jesus and to our own roots in Judaism.

It is very important for us not to forget this or fail to give it sufficient weight. What religion was Jesus? We sometimes forget that he was Jewish. But the New Testament is quite plain: Jesus was born and raised a Jew. He was circumcised on the eighth day, presented in the Temple, and taught in the synagogue. Our first reading today was from the Hebrew scriptures, the Jewish Bible. When I say, "The Lord be with you," it is a Jewish greeting. Our Mass has the Jewish feast of *Pesach* (Passover) as its antecedent. We use unleavened bread for communion because Jesus used *matzoh*. The chalice was once the *Kiddush* cup, the cup of blessing; and the Eucharistic prayer itself is an elaboration of the *berakah*, the Hebrew grace before meals.

It is important for us to see how deeply our own faith and so many of our prayer practices are rooted in the faith of Israel. Of course, there are striking differences. Most central is that we know Jesus not simply as the rabbi from Nazareth but as our Lord and savior. We accept him as Messiah and Son of God. But we don't know him very well if we fail to know him as a Jew.

In today's gospel Jesus summarizes the *Torah* for us in the twin commandments of love of God and love of neighbor. "Hear, O Israel, the Lord is God, the Lord alone. Therefore you shall love the Lord your God with all your heart, with all your soul, with all your mind, and with all your strength." That is the Hebrew way of saying, "You must love God totally." The love of God is logically prior and it is an absolute demand. But in actuality, it must always be demonstrated in the concrete. It must be put into practice by the observance of the second commandment: "You must love your neighbor as yourself." Without the addition of the second command, love of neighbor, the first can hardly be said to exist.

These two commandments are straight out of the

Hebrew scriptures, the books of Deuteronomy and Leviticus. Jesus is drawing on his Hebrew tradition in bringing forth this teaching. He may have been original in connecting the love of God and love of neighbor in this unified way. He was certainly unique in exemplifying it in his life, death and resurrection. For the passion of Christ is not just an example of love, a model for us to copy — we believe it is our salvation. It affects us as profoundly as people can be changed and affected by anything.

Above all, let us not forget what we say in the creed about the death of Christ. "For our sake he was crucified." It was for our sins and the sins of all men and women that Jesus died. The events that brought about our salvation must never be twisted and used as a pretext for anti-Semitism. To do that would be to distort their meaning, to evade the sentence of judgment which the cross passes on each and every one of us, and to show scorn to Jesus, Mary, Joseph and the apostles who were of course all Jewish.

The summary of the law helps us to see distilled in a few sentences what our task as Christians is: the love of God and neighbor. At the same time it helps us to appreciate our roots in the faith of Israel, in the law of Moses, in the very commandments Christ came not to destroy but to fulfill. Let us ask the Lord to help us to know his commands and do them. So may he say of us, "You are not far from the reign of God."

Thirty-Second Sunday of Ordinary Time: Living on the edge

". . . but she gave from her want, all that she had to live on."

The two stories about the generosity of widows from 1 Kings and from St. Mark make quite an eloquent point about poverty of spirit and dependence on God. The widow is a familiar figure in the Bible. She represents the person who is without resources or protection, left alone and at the mercy of any who would take advantage of her. She is seen not simply in the bitterness of grief and desolation over the loss of her spouse, but as exposed to the cruelty of the world in every zone of life. And yet the women whose stories are told in today's scripture are able alternately to offer lavish hospitality to the prophet of God and to give her last dime to the Temple treasury.

Clearly these are extraordinary women, extraordinary human beings. Their gestures are dramatic and compelling. They exemplify heroic courage and a profound trust in God. Like Francis of Assisi, like Jesus himself, they make transparent the kingdom of God. In them grace shines brightly, shines straight through the haze of human misery and gloom that chokes our life and spirit.

Such thrilling examples as these widows, as Francis, *il poverello*, as Jesus, "who emptied himself and became poor," are ever necessary for us. They shock us out of our mediocrity simply because, unlike most of us, they have risked all and live on the outer edges of life. Out on the margins there are no guard rails and no safety nets. No props, no security blankets. No insurance policy, no hedged bet. Only faith sustains and supports them.

But what are we to do? Where is poverty of spirit and reliance on God for us? Our commitment to our spouses, our families, our work, our daily necessities remove any such extravagant gestures from our range of possibilities. Not for most of us the flight to the desert, the selling of all possessions, the renunciation of the world; and necessarily so. For the most part, you and I are already where God wants us to be. So we must discover in the midst of all this complexity the simple way, the little way, the way of peace and detachment.

If, unlike the widow of Zarephath, we shall not give away our last meal, then let us at least place our tiny host on the paten, for it represents our whole life and everything we have. If, unlike Francis, we shall not be casting off our fine clothes in the presence of the bishop, we can at least go before God in the nakedness of our prayer. We can say with the psalmist, "In the secret of my heart teach me wisdom." We can say: Show me, O God, how I need you utterly. Convince me again of your tender mercies, and that you are my all. Let me see what is truly important midst the noise and clutter of my life. In your deep silence shows me my heart's true desire.

> For the Lord keeps faith forever.
> The Lord sets captives free.
> The fatherless and the widow he sustains.
> Praise the Lord, my soul!

Thirty-Third Sunday of Ordinary Time: When the saints go marchin' in

*"But the wise shall shine brightly
like the splendor of the firmament."*

Each November, when the light is failing and the chill winds blow, when the liturgical year is winding down and Advent again draws near, the Church plays its solemn, apocalyptic mood music to turn our thoughts to the world which is to come. Today there is read out to us from scripture the prophetic warning of cosmic peril and imminent danger. The end times, a *leitmotiv* accompanied by modal harmonies and dark orchestration, like the theme of a great symphony, is once again announced.

These dramatic, one may even say sensational, passages can provoke various reactions in us. There is a certain type of personality which takes all of this with utmost seriousness, revels in it, becomes entirely absorbed by the details, by the storm and stress. Such souls are very fond of the religious version of horror movies. For them no amount of bad news and threats of divine retribution is ever enough. They regard the world as an evil place, too

128

full of sinners who laugh off their dire warnings and predictions. But the fact is that such people are more captured by the ghastly details than the big picture. They love to worry, and apocalyptic is their unlimited gift certificate to the candy store.

On the other hand, there are those also who regard such readings as quaint yet faintly embarrassing. In their sophistication they feel that these warnings may have served to keep the wayward in line and cast holy fear into the rubes and bumpkins of another day, but cannot be given serious consideration in this "modern" world. They regard it all as a bit of Halloween foolery, the theological equivalent to dressing up and yelling "boo." But it has no meaning for them because the end of the world is not an idea they dally over.

There is a middle way. We may read these passages seriously, find meaning in them, and see their connection to our life, without getting derailed by the lurid details.

Today's reading from the book of Daniel, similar parts of the Old Testament, the section of Mark's gospel read today, the parallel passages in Matthew and Luke, and above all the book of Revelation are all examples of a kind of writing called apocalyptic or vision literature. It may seem like warmed-over Stephen King but it serves a most important purpose in the Bible. Apocalyptic is a complex mosaic of many hues. Typically it comprises the retelling of historical events, often disasters, the narration of present-day tribulations, and somewhat more indefinite projections about what lies ahead. The landscape thus painted is meant to have familiar references, but with deliberate distortions rather like a surrealist painting. Imagine apocalyptic as a video by Salvador Dali.

Yet apocalyptic is not really meant to terrify. It is addressed to a community already terrified, a community beset with problems, persecuted, whose very survival is a question. The fire and brimstone is for recognition. It affirms God's acknowledgment of their affliction. It says, "You are being crushed in the eyes of the world, but in God's eyes you are winning. When all is revealed in the new age, you will be seen as those who triumphed, but only if you remain faithful. So do not lose heart."

Apocalyptic is meant to lift the spirit. It offers us a grander and a longer view. It takes us beyond our normal and important planning questions. The long view here is not what kind of life insurance should I buy? Not how much will my IRA yield at age 65? Not where will I spend my retirement, but how will I spend eternity? The long view here is, what happens after I die? What happens when the world ends for me?

Scripture shows us that the travail and the pain which we experience now are but the birth pangs of the new creation. It makes us look up from the mud of the trenches where we slog it out day by day. It lifts us toward the sun breaking through the clouds, and toward the future which will be immeasurably better. Yet, it means an end, the end of the world, and we always fear that. But it signals a new beginning:

> [You] will see the Son of Man coming in the clouds with great power and glory. He will dispatch his messengers and assemble his chosen from the four winds, from the farthest bounds of earth and sky.

Here there is nothing fearsome, and everything glorious; nothing to lose and everything to gain. Only, in the words of the spiritual, "Lord, I want to be in that number, when the saints go marchin' in." Or in the words of today's psalm:

> You will show me the path to life,
> fullness of joys in your presence,
> the delights at your right hand forever.
> Keep me safe, O God; you are my hope.

Thirty-Fourth Sunday of Ordinary Time: Christ the King: On the divine names

"The Lord is king, in splendor robed."

Names tell us a lot, and they are a source of endless fascination. For example, many surnames reveal what some distant ancestor did for a living. Once upon a time the Smiths were metal workers; the Coopers made barrels; the Chandlers made candles or were ships' provisioners.

Names tell us who our ancestors were and where they came from. My name, Hanson, is ultimately Scandinavian and is a patronymic. The original Hanson (or Hansson) was "the son of Hans," that is, John. That system has died out in Scandinavia except for some remote rural areas. If it were in force my name ought to be Donald Williamson, because my father is William. And if I had a son and named him Olav, he'd be Olav Donaldson. And my daughter would be Inge Donaldsdotter. (The poor kid!)

Names tell us what people were famous for. Charlemagne means Charles the Great. And his sons were called Charles the Bald, Louis the Pious and Lothair. I guess Lothair didn't have much personality. Better that than being remembered as Ethelred the Unready. Philip the Fair must have been good-looking. And the medieval hymn writer, Hermanus Contractus, shows us by his name that he was a cripple — Herman the Lame.

In the Bible, as you well know, names are very important. Adam names all the animals, to show his part in creation. People get a new name when they are given some special job by God. Thus Abram becomes Abraham; Saul becomes Paul; and Simon becomes Cephas or Peter.

In the Middle Ages an important source for theological reflection was meditating on names. *De nominibus divinis* (On the divine names) was the reflection on how God is called and therefore known. The way Jesus is called in the Bible helps us to understand him. I am struck by the number of titles and images for Jesus there are in today's scripture.

In the first reading, Daniel calls him "one like a son of man." He is thinking of the Messiah, but the Church understands it of Jesus, because that is how Jesus often refers to himself, "the Son of Man." This name reminds us of his incarnation which is the beginning of our salvation.

In the second reading he is called "the faithful witness." The Greek word for witness gives us our English word martyr. Indeed Jesus tells us he came "to bear witness to the truth." And the saints we call martyrs are those who witnessed to him with their very lives.

Jesus is also called "the first-born from the dead." To say "first-born" is to suggest that there are other children to follow. So this is a very hopeful title for us since it suggests that we are to be reborn from death as well.

He is the "ruler of the kings of the earth." That is what our feast is about. Though his kingdom is hidden from the world, it is something we believe in and wait for. His kingdom is not of this world but will transform this world.

Jesus is called the "Alpha and the Omega," that is, "A to Z," the beginning and the end. He is "the one who is, who was and who will be," the Lord of time and history; the "Almighty," which is a divine title. He is God.

Finally, in the gospel, he is seen as the "king," though not in the way that Pilate imagines. On this feast we hail him as our king and the Lord of our lives. God has ruled from the tree and our king wears a crown of thorns. So we are disciples of a crucified master. But we believe that the tree of death has become the cross of victory; and our king lives for ever.

I leave you with a question. How do you think of Jesus? How do you call him in your prayer? You have a wide range to choose from, and there are many other names as well. Let us ponder the question from an Advent hymn: "Who is the King of Glory? How shall we call him?" Each of us must answer that question.

SAINTS AND FEASTS

Presentation of the Lord (February 2):
Casting out the winter dark

*"A revealing light to the Gentiles,
the glory of your people Israel.*

The feast of the Presentation of our Lord in the Temple is the last feast of the Christmas cycle because it celebrates the dedication of Jesus by his parents on the fortieth day after his birth. Anciently it was called in England "Candlemas," because the blessing of church candles took place with a procession, as is still done. So the theme of this celebration is light, both because of this blessing of candles and because of the reading of the gospel in which Simeon calls Jesus "a revealing light to the Gentiles."

The theme is light, also I believe, because of the weak winter light in February. T.S. Eliot says, "April is the cruelest month," but February seems the coldest and darkest. And so our ancestors in the faith who lived in Northern Europe, perhaps co-opting a pagan revel, decided to turn up the lights today and have a little walk-about just to show that the winter dark wasn't going to get them down, and that there was an inner light, the light of Christ, that guided them through the winter of life.

The little baby who is presented in the temple, who is offered by Mary and cradled by Simeon, was also destined to die, and be raised up on the third day and live forever. Because of the promise of this life, a promise he will not see in this world, Simeon can die in peace. Because of the path that lies before this child, a path yet hidden from her, Mary's heart will be pierced with a sword of sorrow.

133

Was it worth it? Would Mary, knowing the pain that she would endure at the foot of the cross, still say yes to God? Would she who is called "blessed among women" spurn the title "mother of sorrows"? The answer is the story unfolded in the gospel.

We light candles today. And candles are fragile lights. The wind may blow them out, and soon enough, when they have given up their wax, they go out. But now they "mingle with the lights of heaven, and continue bravely burning to dispel the darkness of this night!"* Just so, God emptied himself and became poor. He took the form of a servant and was presented as a baby in a temple. He became vulnerable and offered himself on the altar of the cross and was sacrificed for us all. He became our light in darkness, our candle, and shared his light with us. "May this Morning Star which never sets find this flame still burning. [May] Christ, that Morning Star, who came back from the dead shed his peaceful light on all . . . Amen."*

*Easter Vigil: *Exsultet*

Annunciation (March 25):
The Flemish maiden

"Mary said: 'I am the maidservant of the Lord.
Let it be done to me as you say.' "

I tend to picture today's gospel scene in the way the Flemish primitives painted it in countless *Annunciations*, knowing full well that it was nothing like that. For the house in Nazareth could scarcely look like a 15th-century Dutch house, and Mary was no *burgermeester*'s daughter. But it matters not, so long as one has an image that will do, and this image will do nicely.

The Flemish masters, like Hans Memling and Rogier

van der Weyden, always paint Our Lady with a very serene aspect. They paint her as a contemplative, always present in the center of the picture but at the same time a little detached from her surroundings. She is always very beautiful, with fine features, pale skin and dark, lovely eyes. But it is a kind of haunted beauty. These renditions of the Annunciation are always formally posed, according to the style, but more, there is a certain coolness evident in the pose and above all in the facial expression of the Virgin. She is showing humility, but it also seems that she is able to see what her *fiat*, her "yes" will mean, and what it will cost.

When we hear this story, the narration of the Annunciation, it is quite familiar. It strikes us as noble and we hear it gladly, but we do not always consider the human feelings that it represents. For me the Flemish paintings are a way past this block. I do not speak as an art historian, but simply as a viewer and as one who wishes to place himself in that gospel scene. For we come to know Mary in this scene as an unsophisticated village girl. She is not a theologian. She is not an important person, but rather, in the eyes of the world, a nobody. She is not yet the Queen of Heaven whom we honor now with our hymns, but she is about to become the first Christian and the mother of our Lord. For this quiet moment was to become one of history's turning points. Yet it happens not in a Parliament or court room, not on a battlefield or in a stadium, but in the back room of a peasant cottage in a dusty village in an obscure backwater of an empire which long ago ceased to exist.

Mary had no resources at her command — no education, no money, no earthly talents that we know of — save simple faith, a deep humility and a fearless heart. All she had was herself and that is what she gave, just herself, but her entire self. And that is what makes her great.

This is the woman we meet in the gospel, and who looks out at us from those old paintings. Let us pray to her, she who is still called in Flanders by her courtly title *onze lieve vrouw*, "our dear lady." May she bring us to Christ as she brought Christ to us. May she look upon us

with those haunted eyes of pity, and help us to receive
her son at his coming. May he take flesh in our hearts by
our own *fiat*, our faithful "yes."

Solemnity of Saints Peter and Paul (June 29):
Words from prison

*"The Lord will continue to rescue [us] from all
attempts to do us harm, and will bring [us] safe
to his heavenly kingdom."*

This reflection is entitled "Words from prison," because I
want to share with you some of the writings and experiences of four men who "did time." Two of them were ancient,
St. Peter (whose exciting jailbreak is recounted in the first
reading) and St. Paul (who speaks to us in the second reading from house arrest in Rome). Two are modern, Pastor
Dietrich Bonhoeffer and Father Alfred Delp. Prison writings seem to be a compelling though regrettably all too frequent form of literature in the 20th century.

Dietrich Bonhoeffer was a Lutheran pastor and
theologian who was active against the Nazis and an op-
ponent of the co-opted German state church during
World War II. It was thus that he was imprisoned and
finally hanged by the Nazis at the Flossenbürg concentra-
tion camp a few days before it was liberated by the Allies.
He was a man of deep faith, whose faith became clearer
and stronger in the adversity of his confinement.
Bonhoeffer's *Letters and Papers from Prison* reveal this. In
1943 he wrote:

> I believe that God can and will bring good out of evil,
> even out of the greatest evil. For that purpose he needs
> men who make the best use of everything. I believe
> that God will give us all the strength we need to help
> us resist in all times of distress. But he never gives it in

advance, lest we should rely on ourselves and not on him alone. A faith such as this should allay all our fears for the future. I believe that even our mistakes and shortcomings are turned to good account, and that it is no harder for God to deal with them than with our supposedly good deeds. I believe that God is no timeless fate, but that he waits for and answers sincere prayers and responsible actions. (p. 11)

Another man of faith also imprisoned and executed by the Gestapo was Alfred Delp, whose only crime was that he was and wanted to remain a Jesuit priest. Father Delp's *Prison Meditations* are a series of reflections on the Church year made in the naked, truth-telling light of impending death. You would think that a man writing in such circumstances might sound hopeless, tragic and morose. Rather it is courage, tranquility and peace which show through. After receiving the verdict of the trumped-up court he wrote:

Up to now the Lord has helped me wonderfully. I am not yet scared and not yet beaten. The hour of human weakness will no doubt come, and sometimes I am depressed when I think of the things I hoped to do. But I am now a man internally free and far more genuine and realized than I was before. Only now I have sufficient insight to see the thing as a whole. (pp. 161-2)

It was like that for St. Peter, who doubtless wondered whether the Lord would rescue him, and thought when it was happening that it was a mirage. But Peter "recovered his senses," and declared, "Now I know for certain that the Lord has sent his angel to rescue me." St. Paul also, in chains and under the shadow of execution, testifies, "The Lord stood by my side and gave me strength. . . . The Lord will continue to rescue me from all attempts to do me harm and will bring me safe to his heavenly kingdom."

There are many prisons, not only the civil jails in which those who have been convicted of crime are kept.

There are, as well, the prisons in which students, union activists and other "prisoners of conscience" have "disappeared"; prisons in which women and children are subjected to unspeakable and sadistic brutality; prisons where the only crime is to have been a poet whose words are "inconvenient" to the regime. And there are, as well, prisons that have no walls or bars or moats. Prisons within; prisons of the mind and emotions; prisons of the spirit and the flesh. There is the prison of hatred and fear; of prejudice, envy and lust. The prison of lies; of murder, violence and revenge. There is finally the prison of death.

All of these prisons — which the New Testament sums up in the single word *hamartia*, or "Sin" (with a capital "S") — all of them can be broken out of. Christ who lay in the shackles of death has broken his bonds and released us all from prison. The door has swung open and now we are free — free from sin and free from death's bitter pangs; free to speak and act in behalf of justice; free to remember the names of those whom society would forget; free to feel compassion and demonstrate it; free to change ourselves and our society. So let us seize freedom and rejoice, for "the Lord will continue to rescue us from all attempts to do us harm, and will bring us safe to his heavenly kingdom."

Transfiguration (August 6): ". . . like shining from shook foil"

"He was transfigured before their eyes and his clothes became dazzlingly white — whiter than the work of any bleacher could make them."

It is the presence of God, the intimate presence of the most holy and infinite God, that the disciples experience on top of the mountain. The transfiguration of Christ is

138

for them a transforming encounter with God, a mystical experience. By mystical I do not mean unreal, quite the contrary. Such experiences, which are neither hallucinations nor the result of a psychotic state, are perhaps the most deeply real events in our lives. Nor are they rare or reserved only for great saints and contemplatives. What happened to the disciples atop the mountain was a decisive step in their spiritual journey and has doubtless been preserved in the gospel to be a landmark for us.

God is present to us at all times and in many ways: in the wonder of creation, the beauty of the world, the love of a friend, in prayer and sacrament, in word of salvation, whether in the Bible or spoken by a fellow Christian. But sometimes, as Gerard Manley Hopkins puts it, the presence of God "will flame out, like shining from shook foil." That doesn't happen every day, but it does occur every now and then. Many can testify to times when God seemed especially close, when they felt themselves surrounded by a presence both compelling and fearful, in which one seemed terribly, terribly small yet at the same time wonderfully buoyed up by love. Sometimes it is so intense that one may feel the joy of it cannot be contained and the heart is near to bursting. Poetry wells up inside, yet words are quite useless. All that is necessary then is to sit quietly and be absorbed by the presence. At the same time one knows that as this sojourn in heaven is brief, one must be especially attentive, so as to make the most of the moment and be faithful to the grace that is given.

It is something like this that the disciples experience when Jesus takes them up the mountain. In the Bible it is always to the mountain that one goes to encounter God. They go up with Jesus and something happens that words cannot describe. Their language in description of it is highly symbolic because the reality itself is ineffable; it may not be spoken. It is something like bright light, not just an outer light but a light that shone from within Jesus so that his appearance is changed. The disciples are reported to have fallen asleep. Perhaps they fainted; perhaps they experienced some sort of amnesia or ecstasy. Whatever transpired has affected them in deeper parts of their personality than just their conscious minds. When the figures accompanying Jesus, whom they recognize as Moses and Elijah, begin to go away they try to prevent it. Peter babbles something about building tents. He doesn't know what to say; he just doesn't want it to end. Next they speak of being in a cloud and enshrouded with mist. The enveloping darkness, in contrast to the bright light at the beginning, is fearful. They hear a voice testifying of Jesus "my Son, my Chosen One. Listen to him."

That this strange and wonderful encounter serves a purpose and has meaning beyond itself is without doubt. Luke has left his fingerprints and many other clues all over the passage. First, it follows Peter's confession of faith, a keystone in the architecture of the gospel, and Jesus' prediction of the passion. Next, Moses and Elijah, who represent the Law and the prophets, speak about "the 'passage' which [Jesus] is about to fulfill in Jerusalem." In Greek this word "passage" is *exodus*. It means departure; clearly, it means death. But for Luke it has a twofold reference. It looks back to the book of Exodus which describes the first Passover, and forward to the paschal mission of Christ, his suffering, death and resurrection. St. Leo the Great brings all of this into focus in one of his sermons. "The great reason for this transfiguration," he says, "was to remove the scandal of the cross from the hearts of [Jesus'] disciples, and to prevent the humiliation of his voluntary suffering from disturbing the faith of those who had witnessed the surpassing glory that lay concealed."

The transfiguration teaches us to treasure those moments when God makes his presence sweetly felt in our hearts and impresses his glory on our minds. Whether we have felt that presence most intensely in an experience of prayer, or a moment of forgiveness and liberation, or in the tender love of a spouse, or however it was given, we must remember and cherish it. We must cultivate the memory of it, rehearse it in our meditation, live by it in our comings and goings, our work and our leisure. For it is just there in our inward being that Jesus has written his name. It is from there, from that fixed and familiar point within our soul, within our memory and imagination, where dwell Father, Son and Spirit. From there we shall draw strength to go on in difficult days. When the dark cloud surrounds us, the "cloud of unknowing," it will be within this inner chamber, this secret place of our heart that we can pick up the trail that leads back to God.

Assumption of the Blessed Virgin Mary (August 15): In the hope of heaven

"Christ the first fruits and then, at his coming, all those who belong to him."

On a hot and sticky August day the Church wants to make us think of heaven. Our thoughts will likely not be in heaven today. They will be leaden, weighed down by summer heat. Yet it is good for us to stretch ourselves as far as we can in heaven's way, for when the weather is heavy we become all the more burdened by our "too, too solid flesh." We feel the oppression of the heat and become downhearted. We need our spirits restored and our sights raised.

This feast makes us think of heaven because it celebrates Mary's going there. In the words of the solemn definition of the dogma, the idea is this: It was fitting that the mother of our Lord, "when the course of her earthly life was finished, [should be] taken up body and soul into the glory of heaven." There is nothing surprising in that; it is the way we think of our Lady all the time.

But the point is that we are supposed to think that way about ourselves. We are supposed to nurture a deep hope of heaven in our hearts. We must begin to see Mary, not as so extraordinarily different from us and far above, but as one of us who has made good and now shows us the way. This feast is not meant to frustrate us by making heaven feel remote, but to encourage us to see it as really possible, even probable (given all the help that God offers).

Trouble is, most of us were brought up to be more than a little bashful about harboring aspirations to sanctity or making idle claims to a reserved seat in heaven. The conception of the spiritual life portrayed to recent generations was that of a minefield in which every possible trap was set to bring down not only the truly wicked, but also the merely careless, and the simply foolish (among whom we certainly numbered ourselves).

The mentality we absorbed was not that of going to heaven, but of trying to stay out of hell. Mortal sin was something one "fell into" like a pothole. We thought of ourselves as sinners in a silly and pathetic way, more or less like being accident prone or susceptible to earaches. We prayed, not to know a foretaste of heaven's joys, but that a priest would be there to snatch us from Satan's clutches just in the nick of time. No one ever spoke to us confidently of our salvation, or did so only rarely.

But when we read the New Testament we discover that "saint" is the word which describes every Christian, you and me. And that the call to discipleship is something offered to each one of us, individually and personally. And that there is no such thing in the Church as a class of people who are "professionally holy." There is a sacrament of holy orders, to be sure, but not all are holy who are in orders, and many are the saints whose names are never printed in the liturgical calendar. This is not to deny that holiness is a life-long struggle, or that the saints we honor on their feast days were not true heroes or heroines of the faith. It is simply to assert that holiness is for everyone and heaven is meant to begin now.

Our Lady teaches us this. Mary did not become a saint on the day God took her to heaven. Mary became a saint on the day she visited Elizabeth in a tiny village in the hill country of Judah. Mary became a saint when she said yes to God in the person of an angel. Mary became a saint when she cooked and cleaned and changed diapers. Mary became a saint when she stood by her dying Son. In these things she is very like to us. And today we pray that we may be very like to her.

All Saints (November 1): God's children now

"Who do you think these are, all dressed in white?"

Today's feast makes us think about something we likely spend little time thinking about: sanctity, sainthood, holiness — not only asking the intercession of the saints but aspiring to join them, trying to become one in our own right.

When I was small the saints always seemed so far away to me, first of all, because they are dead. They are dead and safe in heaven, but here I am alive and in the thick of it here on earth. Then too, the saints appeared to be fairy-tale characters, far removed from modern life. One or two Maria Gorettis or Dominic Savios could not make up for the legions of ancient apostles and medieval monks so alien to a child of the 'fifties. But above all, it was the feeling that they were so far above me. They were heroes and heroines, larger than life. They were ten feet tall, legendary, and here I was so ordinary. Nothing in my life could remotely compare to the drama of facing the lions in the amphitheater or preaching to the heathens who would pop you into their pot and have you for dinner.

But the great glory about today, about All Saints, is that it says you don't have to be famous to be a saint. You don't have to be a storybook character. You don't have to have written the most famous book in all the history of theology. The only vows you need take are the baptismal ones your parents and godparents pronounced on the day of your baptism. It's not that I don't appreciate the great saints, the famous ones who've all got their own feast days. It's just that this day is for all the rest of us, to cheer us on and spur us to greater efforts, or at least to clap us on the back and say, "Look kid, don't quit now!"

Truth to tell, some of the famous saints were pretty ordinary too. Some were just everyday workers and housewives and priests like you and me. But others were pretty odd. Some were crazy as loons, and some had such angular personalities that they had to go off and become hermits or their friends would have surely killed them. Some were reluctant saints, dragged to holiness kicking and screaming at the last possible moment; others were perfectly adjusted and appeared to be holy from the first. None of them wore halos; few, if any, could play the harp; and most, I guess, would be dismayed by the way they are depicted on holy cards.

What they all had in common was this. God called them to be saints, and God accomplished saintliness in them. Sainthood is God's business in the first place, not ours. But all of them cooperated with God, or at least stopped fighting him in the end. So there's hope for us.

The saints are simply those who came near to living that life which the gospel describes to us, the life of the beatitudes. They were men and women, boys and girls, in whom some echo of Jesus' voice could be heard, some feature of his face could be seen. They were just like us but they were something more. And that something more is what we pray about today. Let us ask that we can have that something more. Let us ask that God will make us saints too.

All Souls (November 2): In the communion of saints

"Father, all those you gave me I would have in my company where I am, to see this glory of mine which is your gift to me."

All Souls is a day of mixed emotions. It is sadness mixed with hope and memories mingled with a promise. We pray for the dead. And we count on Jesus' gospel prayer and make it our own: "Father, all those you gave me I would have in my company where I am, to see this glory of mine, which is your gift to me."

That is our theme, but there is not much glory in All Souls Day itself. There is none of the triumph and rejoicing of All Saints. All Souls is rather more quiet, more modest, more poignant. There is about it a certain wistfulness, a certain sadness. It is the sadness of our mortality, which the Roman poet Vergil so aptly puts:

Sunt lacrimae rerum et mentem mortalia tangunt.

Here are the tears of things,
and what is mortal touches the heart.

For us it is not death in the abstract that we come to contemplate today. It is death at its most personal and particular with which we contend. It is death the thief who has snatched away our loved ones. Death the robber who has claimed all the names written the envelopes placed on the altar. Those names are full of memories for us, and full of heartaches and sighs.

But they are also full of beauty, full of smiles, full of love. Those names made us who we are. Those names handed on the faith to us. Those names taught us how to pray, and call us to prayer today. For what we do today is prompted by the deepest conviction that, though they are beyond our reach, yet can we be in touch with them. Though we cannot converse with them, we can really help them.

Our All Souls Day Mass is founded in our conviction of the Creed, in the articles on "the resurrection of the body" and "the communion of saints." Because we believe in these two things — that we shall rise again, and that even now we have solidarity with the saints and the poor souls — because we believe that, we can pray today. It is this faith which allows us to escape the futility which trapped the poet. And it is this faith which allows us to escape the self-pity in which hopeless mourning can imprison us.

We pray with hope, knowing that though we are weak and sinful, Jesus is strong, and will not fail in his purpose to bring his beloved into his company. We know that the Father's love for him will live in us and in the souls of those for whom we pray. We pray in the conviction that nothing can separate us from the love of Christ, not even death. We pray knowing that God who justifies will not condemn his faithful ones, and that Jesus intercedes for us at the right hand of God.

God assures us with his holy word and gives us the earnest of it in the sacrament. For this sacred meal is a rehearsal of the banquet we shall share with all saints and all souls in the kingdom. One of the prayers "over the gifts" says, "We are united in this sacrament by the love of Jesus Christ." And I believe the "we" in question is not just the "we" who are standing around the altar but also those who have gone before us in faith. The love of Christ unites us. May his love preserve us and keep us all unto life everlasting. Amen.

(Suggested readings: Daniel 12:1-3; Romans 8:31-35, 37-39; John 17:24-26)

Immaculate Conception (December 8): The new Eve

"Rejoice, O highly favored daughter! The Lord is with you."

Today we celebrate the Immaculate Conception of the Blessed Virgin Mary. In so doing we are telling the story of Mary and singing her song. We discover that we cannot do that without telling our own story and singing Christ's song, a hymn of praise to our God.

In the words of the solemn definition of 1854, the Immaculate Conception means that "the Most Blessed Virgin Mary from the first moment of her conception was, by the singular grace and privilege of Almighty God, in view of the merits of Jesus Christ the Savior of the human race, preserved immune from all stain of original sin. . . ."

This teaching reflects the imagery of the Bible's stories of creation and redemption. Thus, Mary is the new Eve. By the disobedience of Adam and Eve sin entered the world. By contrast, through the obedience of Mary the savior of the world is born. The Hebrew name Eve (*hawah*) means "mother of all the living" (Gn 3:20). Just so, Mary is the "mother of the Church" and the model of faith. She is the first of the redeemed.

In all of this our story is told. For the obedience of Mary and her cooperation with God's plan show that God is greater than our sin, and is not thwarted by our crooked hearts. Mary, like all the baptized, was, in the words of St. Paul, predestined for adoption and the first to hope in Christ. In their liturgy the Cistercian monks call Mary the *fenestra coeli*, the "window of heaven." Through her we see a glimpse of what awaits us. And from her place in heaven she intercedes for us and encourages us.

So these stories are all intertwined: Christ's and Mary's and ours. Saint Anselm sums it up in the lesson that is read in the Liturgy of the Hours for today's feast:

God, then, is the Father of the created world and Mary the mother of the recreated world. God is the Father by whom all things were given life, and Mary the mother through whom all things were given new life. For God begot the Son, through whom all things were made, and Mary gave birth to him as the Savior of the world. Without God's Son, nothing could exist; without Mary's Son, nothing could be redeemed.

Index of Scriptural Readings for the Sundays and Feasts Year B

ADVENT THROUGH CHRISTMAS SEASONS

1 Adv.: Is 63:16b-17, 19b; 64:2b-7. 1 Cor 1:3-9. Mk 13:33-37
2 Adv.: Is 40:1-5, 9-11. 2 Pt 3:8-14. Mk 1:1-8
3 Adv.: Is 61:1-2a, 10-11. 1 Thes 5:16-24. Jn 1:6-8, 19-28
4 Adv.: 2 Sm 7:1-6, 8b-11, 16. Rom 16:25-27. Lk 1:26-38
CHRISTMAS:
    Vigil: Is 62:1-5. Acts 13:16-17, 22-25. Mt 1:1-25
    Midnight: Is 9:1-6. Ti 2:11-14. Lk 2:1-14
    Dawn: Is 62:11-12. Ti 3:4-7. Lk 2:15-20
    Day: Is 52:7-10. Heb 1:1-6. Jn 1:1-18
Holy Family: Sir 3:2-6, 12-14. Col 3:12-21. Lk 2:22-40
Epiphany: Is 60:1-6. Eph 3:2-3a, 5-6. Mt 2:1-12
Baptism of the Lord: Is 42:1-4, 6-7. Acts 10:34-38. Mk 1:6b-11

LENT THROUGH EASTER SEASONS

Ash Wed.: Jl 2:12-18. 2 Cor 5:20 — 6:2. Mt 6:1-6, 16-18
1 Lent: Gn 9:8-15. 2 Pt 3:18-22. Mk 1:12-15
2 Lent: Gn 22:1-2, 9a, 10-13, 15-18. Rom 8:31b-34. Mk 9:2-10
3 Lent: Ex 20:1-17. 1 Cor 1:22-25. Jn 2:13-25
4 Lent: 2 Chr 36:14-16, 19-23. Eph 2:4-10. Jn 3:14-21
5 Lent: Jer 31:31-34. Heb 5:7-9. Jn 12:20-33
Passion Sunday: Is 50:4-7. Phil 2:6-11. Mk 14:1 — 15:47
Holy Thursday: Ex 12:1-8, 11-14. 1 Cor 11:23-26. Jn 13:1-15
Good Friday: Is 52:13 — 53:12. Heb 4:14-16, 5:7-9. Jn 18:1 — 19:42
Easter Sunday: Acts 10:34a, 37-43. Col 3:1-4, or 1 Col 5:6b-8. Jn 20:1-9, or Mk 16:1-8. Evening 3 - Lk 24:13-35
2 Easter: Acts 4:32-35. 1Jn 5:1-6. Jn 20:19-31
3 Easter: Acts 3:13-15, 17-19. 1Jn 2:1-5a. Lk 24:35-48
4 Easter: Acts 4:8-12. 1 Jn 3:1-2. Jn 10:11-18
5 Easter: Acts 9:26-31. 1 Jn 3:18-24. Jn 15:1-8
6 Easter: Acts 10:25-26, 34-35, 44-48. 1 Jn 4:7-10. Jn 15:9-17
Ascension: Acts 1:1-11. Eph 1:17-23. Mk 16:15-20
7 Easter: Acts 1:15-17, 20a, 20c-26. 1 Jn 4:11-16. Jn 17:11b-19
Pentecost: Acts 2:1-11. 1 Cor 12:3b-7, 12-13. Jn 20:19-23

SEASON OF THE YEAR (ORDINARY TIME)

Trinity Sunday: Dt 4:32-34, 39-40. Rom 8:14-17. Mt 28:16-20
Corpus Christi: Ex 24:3-8. Heb 9:11-15. Mk 14:12-16, 22-26
2 Ord.: 1 Sm 3:3b-10, 19. 1 Cor 6:13c-15a, 17-20. Jn 1:35-42
3 Ord.: Jon 3:1-5, 10. 1 Cor 7:29-31. Mk 1:14-20
4 Ord.: Dt 18:15-20. 1 Cor 7:32-35. Mk 1:21-28
5 Ord.: Jb 7:1-4, 6-7. 1 Cor 9:16-19, 22-23. Mk 1:29-39
6 Ord.: Lv 13:1-2, 45-46. 1 Cor 10:31 – 11.1. Mk 1:40-45
7 Ord.: Is 43:18-19, 21-22, 24b-25. 2 Cor 1:18-22. Mk 2:1-12
8 Ord.: Hos 2:16b, 17b, 21-22. 2 Cor 3:1b-6. Mk 2:18-22
9 Ord.: Dt 5:12-15. 2 Cor 4:6-11. Mk 2:23 – 3:6
10 Ord.: Gn 3:9-15. 2 Cor 4:13 – 5:1. Mk 3:20-35
11 Ord.: Ez 17:22-24. 2 Cor 5:6-10. Mk 4:26-34
12 Ord.: Jb 38:1, 8-11. 2 Cor 5:14-17. Mk 4:35-41
13 Ord.: Wis 1:13-15, 2:23-24. 2 Cor 8:7, 9, 13-15. Mk 5:21-43
14 Ord.: Ez 2:2-5. 2 Cor 12:7-10. Mk 6:1-6
15 Ord.: Am 7:12-15. Eph 1:3-14. Mk 6:7-13
16 Ord.: Jer 23:1-6. Eph 2:13-18. Mk 6:30-34
17 Ord.: 2 Kgs 4:42-44. Eph 4:1-6. Jn 6:1-15
18 Ord.: Ex 16:2-4, 12-15. Eph 4:17, 20-24. Jn 6:24-35
19 Ord.: 1 Kgs 19:4-8. Eph 4:30 – 5:2. Jn 6:41-45
20 Ord.: Prv 9:1-6. Eph 5:15-20. Jn 6:51-58
21 Ord.: Jos 24:1-2a, 15-17, 18b. Eph 5:21-32. Jn 6:60-69
22 Ord.: Dt 4:1-2, 6-8. Jas 1:17-18, 21b-22, 27. Mk 7:1-8, 14-15, 21-23
23 Ord.: Is 35:4-7a. Jas 2:1-5. Mk 7:31-37
24 Ord.: Is 50:5-9a. Jas 2:14-18. Mk 8:27-35
25 Ord.: Wis 2:12, 17-20. Jas 3:16 – 4:3. Mk 9:30-37
26 Ord.: Nm 11:25-29. Jas 5:1-6. Mk 9:38-43, 45, 47-48
27 Ord.: Gn 2:18-24. Heb 2:9-11. Mk 10:2-16
28 Ord.: Wis 7:7-11. Heb 4:12-13. Mk 10:17-30
29 Ord.: Is 53:10-11. Heb 4:14-16. Mk 10:35-43
30 Ord.: Jer 31:7-9. Heb 5:1-6. Mk 10:46-53
31 Ord.: Dt 6:2-6. Heb 7:23-28. Mk 12:28b-34
32 Ord.: 1 Kgs 17:10-16. Heb 9:24-28. Mk 12:38-44
33 Ord.: Dn 12:1-3. Heb 10:11-14, 18. Mk 13:24-32
Christ the King: Dn 7:13-14. Rv 1:5-8. Jn 18:33b-37

SAINTS AND FEASTS

Presentation (Feb. 2): Mal 3:1-4. Heb 2:14-18. Lk 2:22-40
Annunciation (Mar. 25): Is 7:10-14. Heb 10:4-10. Lk 1:26-38
Sts. Peter and Paul (June 29): Acts 12:1-11. 2 Tm 4:6-8, 17-18. Mt 16:13-19
Assumption (Aug. 15): Rev 11:19 – 12:1-6, 10. 1 Cor 15:20 – 16. Lk 1:39-56
All Saints (Nov. 1): Rev 7:2-4, 9-14. 1 Jn 3:1-3. Mt 5:1-12
All Souls (Nov. 2): Dn 12:1-3. Rom 6:3-9. Jn 6:37-40
Immaculate Conception (Dec. 8): Gn 3:9-15, 20. Eph 1:3-6, 11-12. Lk 1:26-38

Other Resurrection Press Publications

RVC Liturgical Series — brief, easy-to-read books for those actively involved in liturgical ministry or who simply wish to better understand the Catholic liturgy.

No. 1. *Our Liturgy: Your Guide to the Basics* $4.25

No. 2. *The Great Seasons: Your Guide to Celebrating* $3.25

No. 3. *The Liturgy of the Hours: Your Guide to Praying* $3.95

No. 4. *The Lector's Ministry: Your Guide to Proclaiming the Word* $3.25

A Celebration of Life: Catholic Spirituality Today — Anthony T. Padovano

"Spirituality, quite simply, is about meaning and purpose, about whether we count or are accountable, about whether we make a difference or live without significance." In a gentle, meditative style, the author surveys current Catholic spirituality as it touches every facet of our lives. $7.95

Miracle in the Marketplace: Healing and Loving in the Modern World — Henry Libersat

"Here indeed is a call to a renewed sense of lay mission in the world — a mission of presence and service — sent into the world by a parish with a broadened vision of Church." Quiet prayer and reflection on pertinent questions and a commitment to action are built into every chapter. $5.95